MOTORCYCLES
WE LOVED IN THE
1990S

PHIL WEST

The
History
Press

Front cover images, clockwise from left: Yamaha YZF-R1
(Yamaha); Ducati M900 Monster (Ducati); BMW R1150GS (BMW)

Back cover images, top to bottom: Kawasaki's 1990 ZZ-R600 was
one of the most popular entrants into the hugely competitive
super sport 600 category (Kawasaki); Ducati's 1994 916 became
an instant winner in World Supebike racing, first with Carl
Fogarty and later, here, with Troy Bayliss (Ducati)

First published 2024

The History Press
97 St George's Place, Cheltenham,
Gloucestershire, GL50 3QB
www.thehistorypress.co.uk

British Library Cataloguing in Publication Data.
A catalogue record for this book is available from the British Library.

ISBN 978 1 80399 332 4

Typesetting and origination by The History Press
Printed and bound in India by Thomson Press India Ltd

Opposite: If one category of bikes rose to become more
popular and more significant than any other during the
1990s, it was surely the supersport 600. And most popular
of all was Honda's brilliant CBR600F2. (Honda)

The 1990s also saw a return to 'form' for BMW. The German marque's all-new oil-cooled Boxer twin powerplant powered not just the new R1100RS, but its reinvented R1100GS adventure and R1100R roadster. (BMW)

CONTENTS

ABOUT THE AUTHOR

Phil West is one of the UK's best-known and longest-established motorcycle journalists and authors.

His thirty-plus-year career at the top of the profession has included being editor of leading magazines *Bike* and *What Bike* as well as *American Motorcycles* and *Biking Times*. He was also Executive Editor at *Motor Cycle News*. As a freelancer, his work has been published around the globe in publications varying from *Stuff* to *FHM* and the *Evening Standard*, and he remains a regular contributor to *MCN*, *Bike*, *Visordown*, *Autotrader* and others. During this time he has ridden and written about virtually every new bike.

He's also a prolific, successful author of motorcycling books, ranging from acclaimed histories of the Yamaha RD350LC, Honda Gold Wing and BMW GS to the two sister titles to this book, *Motorcycles We Loved in the 1970s* and *Motorcycles We Loved in the 1980s*.

ACKNOWLEDGEMENTS

I would like to thank a few individuals for their help and support in producing this book. My wife, Sarah, yet again for her support, tolerance and the occasional biscuit while I toil away at the keyboard, my late dad for encouraging and facilitating my first forays into publishing and journalism, my late mum whose grasp of English was always better than mine and, finally, Amy Rigg and all at The History Press for having the confidence to help me make this book happen.

INTRODUCTION

For many, the 1990s was one of the greatest motorcycling decades of all.

In bikesport, the new World Superbike Championship (WSB) soared in popularity, highlighting sports bikes such Ducati's 916 and Honda's RC45, and making heroes out of Carl Fogarty and Scott Russell. At the same time 500cc GPs had its golden era as Americans Kevin Schwantz, Wayne Rainey and Eddie Lawson fought toe to two-stroke toe against emerging antipodeans Wayne Gardner and Mick Doohan.

It saw the return of some of biking's most famous brands. In the UK, Triumph came back from the dead; in Italy, Ducati hit the big time while the decade's end saw MV Agusta's almost mythical return.

There was a new way of importing bikes from the Far East. 'Grey imports', where non-official importers filled containers with used examples of mystical Japanese models that would never otherwise come to the UK, allowed a whole generation to sample mouth-watering motorcycles such as Yamaha's TZR250, Suzuki's GSX-R400 and Honda's 'Baby Blade' CBR400RR.

One of the most significant of all 1990s bikes was Honda's revolutionary 1992 CBR900RR FireBlade, the ultra-light and compact sportster that famously 'rewrote the superbike rule book'. (Honda)

There were revolutionary breakthroughs in bike design and style. Honda's 1992 CBR900RR FireBlade famously 'rewrote the superbike rule book' with its emphasis on light weight over brute power. Yamaha's 1998 YZF-R1 then took the concept to the next level; Ducati's 1993 Monster 900 introduced the 'naked' and the 1990s was also the decade of the 'hyperbike' – monstrously powerful speed machines made popular first with 1990's Kawasaki ZZ-R1100 before the mantle was passed, first to Honda's CBR1100XX Super Blackbird then, ultimately, literally, with Suzuki's 200mph 1999 GSX-1300R Hayabusa. Motorcycling would never see such unbridled speed again.

Much of this was only possible by unstinting advances in technology. Although radical design was more prevalent than ever – Honda built its oval-pistoned NR750, Yamaha its hub-centre-steered GTS1000 – it was the more subtle advances that made the greatest difference. Standardised 17in wheels with radial tyres, stiff inverted forks and formulaic aluminium twin beam frames meant Japanese sports bikes handled better than ever. Improvements in materials and a quest for lighter, more compact dimensions made them more manageable.

But it's the bikes themselves that are remembered most fondly and which best illustrate a decade that changed motorcycling forever.

The fifty motorcycles in this book were all hugely loved through the 1990s, due to their technology, style, performance or all-round ability. Some are household names revered by thousands; others were short-lived exotica reserved for an exclusive few, yet still significant for the impact they made. All were loved and lusted after in a decade that formed a generation of bikers. This book hopes to convey exactly why they were so special.

The 1990s were also to herald the end of some bike breeds, most notably two-stroke sports bikes, which were being regulated off the road but reached their pinnacle with the Suzuki RGV250, Kawasaki's KR-1S and, here, Aprilia's RS250. (Aprilia)

SOME KIND OF ULTIMATES

The 1990s saw new biking benchmarks being set not least for outright speed. Kawasaki's new 1990 ZZ-R1100, with 147bhp and capable of 174mph reigned as the world's fastest production motorcycle for the first half of the decade. (Kawasaki)

SUZUKI GSX-R1100L, 1990

1990's new GSX-R1100L was Suzuki's successor to the controversial GSX-R1100K.
It was the first production superbike with the new inverted telescopic forks. (Suzuki)

When it comes to superbikes, if the 1990s would ultimately prove to be a decade of revolutionary change, with radical, nimble lightweights such as Honda's 1992 CBR900RR FireBlade showing a new way to speed, then the ultimate example of the old, heavyweight guard was surely the 1990 Suzuki GSX-R1100L.

The big 'Gixxer' had proved revolutionary when launched in 1986 as the big brother to the lightweight, racer-replica GSX-R750F. But while the '11' had itself been light, powerful and effective, thereafter Suzuki lost its way. In 1988 the 750 gained power, weight and a new look to become the 'Slingshot'. Then in 1989 the 1100 followed suit with extra capacity (1052–1127cc), power (130–138bhp) and bulk (197–210kg) to become, as the GSX-R1100K, one of the most fearsome (and feared) motorcycle monsters of modern times.

Forks apart, it looked almost identical to its predecessor – big, burly and, with 140+bhp, fearsome. But at least the handling had been calmed. (Suzuki)

New forks weren't the only upgrade: the wheelbase was 35mm longer, there was a new rear shock, plus wider tyres, all to aid straight-line stability. (Suzuki)

It couldn't last – and it didn't. Tragic accidents in the Production TT led to the dropping of the class; Suzuki calmed and controlled its beast the following year, and the result, the GSX-R1100L now with a stabilising, longer wheelbase, all-new and much-improved suspension (including the first inverted forks on a production superbike), while still big and blisteringly fast, brought a degree of sanity to the large Suzuki. The 'L' may still not have had the refinement and easy aplomb of its Yamaha rival, the EXUP, and later, facelifted, water-cooled GSX-R11s may have been better technically, but for an effective, hairy-chested, heavyweight, old-school, classically styled GSX-R, the 'L' was surely some kind of ultimate.

WHO LOVED IT?

With 147bhp from its 1,129cc four compared to the rival Yamaha EXUP's 145bhp and 1,002cc, plus an all-up wet weight of 240kg, the GSX-R was the most powerful, biggest, heaviest and most fearsome superbike of all and as a result loved by hooligans, specials builders and streetfighters. As the 'last of the big Gixxers' it still is …

KAWASAKI ZZ-R600, 1990

Kawasaki launched both its new ZZ-Rs in early 1990 but it was the all-new 600, which replaced the GPX600, that grabbed the early headlines. (Kawasaki)

In early 1990 Kawasaki, the Japanese brand whose reputation was founded on 1970s powerhouses such as the Z1, reasserted its claim as speed king with a new prefix: ZZ-R, and not one, but two new machines – the ZZ-R600 and ZZ-R1100.

With both based around improved four-cylinder engines and the biggest power outputs and top speeds in their class, the 99bhp, 153mph 600 succeeded the GPX600, added sports tourer class and was created to be top dog in the most popular and competitive class of all – supersports 600s.

For a while it succeeded. The best-selling 600 of 1990 delivered smooth style, whistlingly fast speed, roomy, cultured comfort, decent handling and a classy refinement that made rivals such as Yamaha's lighter, sportier FZR600 seem basic and raw.

WHAT THEY SAID

'The Kawasaki ZX-6 (as called in the US) is a motorcycle that could get away with a whole lot of evil if it had to just on the merits of its incredible motor. It's a motorcycle designed for the racetrack that street riders will love. It's a hardcore sportbike that's comfortable and versatile.'

Cycle World, March 1990, on the $5,499 Kawasaki ZX-6

The uprated engine was the most powerful in the class, making the ZZ-R the new 600 speed king. A new, roomy, classy chassis, meanwhile, helped make it a brilliant all-rounder. (Kawasaki)

The new ZZ-R600 also handled well enough to be an excellent sportster and on track even won that year's British Supersport championship in the hands of John Reynolds. (Kawasaki)

And while not intended as an out-and-out sportster, that speed and all-round aplomb was also enough for Team Green's John Reynolds to win the UK's 1990 600 Supercup championship.

It wasn't to last, of course. Honda leapfrogged the ZZ-R in 1991 with its new CBR600F2, but the Kawasaki's slick speed and big bike appeal ensured it remained a big seller.

The first ZZ-R600D1 was facelifted and improved into the 1993 E1. And even when relegated into sports tourer status by Kawasaki's new ZX-6R in 1995, the ZZ-R remained popular and appreciated, with a reputation for quality, versatility and reliability enabling it to live on in Kawasaki's line-up right up to 2007. Only its great-grandaddy, the truly legendary 1984–2003 GPz900R, lived longer ...

WHO LOVED IT?

The ZZ-R6 was not only fast, it was bigger than most rival 600s, better equipped, roomier and more comfortable, making it effectively a 750 sports tourer in 600cc form. All of which made it popular and helped it stay in production for seventeen years, by which time it was considered an affordable all-rounder.

KAWASAKI ZZ-R1100, 1990

If Kawasaki's new ZZ-R600 was the tempting appetiser to the new decade, its big brother, the ZZ-R1100, launched at the same press event in the south of France in February 1990, was very much the main event.

Although initially appearing little more than an update of the potent but flawed 1988 ZX-10 (the successor to the GPZ1000RX, itself an unconvincing 1986 upgrade on the

game-changing 1984 GPZ900R), the reality proved revolutionary and would literally set the pace for most of the 1990s.

A 2mm bigger bore added 55cc, taking capacity up to 1,052cc, which, along with a new ram air system, boosted peak power from 137 to a world-leading 147bhp.

An update in 1993 with a new nose and quality and detail changes helped keep the ZZ-R1100 on top until the arrival of Honda's all-new CBR1100XX Super Blackbird in 1996. (Kawasaki)

Although based on the old ZX-10, the new ZZ-R1100 had an all-new, much-improved frame, more power and new aerodynamic bodywork, all helping it become the fastest bike of the day. (Kawasaki)

An all-new, beefy, aluminium twin-spar frame and swingarm succeeded where the ZX-10s had failed in keeping all that power under control and giving a blend of steady stability and calm cornering no 500lb bike had delivered before.

New, wind tunnel-developed bodywork, if not making the ZZ-R exactly beautiful, gave Kawasaki's new flagship both impressive wind-cheating ability and an unmistakably brutish profile few would forget.

And that was just the start. On the test strip, the ZZ-R quickly staked a new speed standard – 174mph, enough for it to be revered as the world's fastest production motorcycle for years to come.

But the way the ZZ-R delivered that speed, from a meaty midrange before the ram air made it seemingly get faster ... and faster – *and faster* was equally impressive. If you wanted the fastest, 'boss-est' big bike of the early 1990s, the ZZ-R1100 was it.

WHO LOVED IT?

The 'world's fastest production motorcycle' was the obvious sales point but the ZZ-R11 was much more than that: the first hyperbike without handling foibles that was a truly useful all-rounder. After the 'first gen' ZZ-R1100C, the improved ZZ-R1100D arrived in 1993 and remained in production right up to 2001.

HARLEY-DAVIDSON FLSTF FAT BOY, 1990

Possibly the most famous movie motorcycle of the 1990s. Arnold Schwarzenegger's Terminator with John Connor (Edward Furlong) flees on a Harley Fat Boy in *Terminator 2: Judgment Day*. (Harley-Davidson)

No Harley made a bigger impact in 1990s movies than the Fat Boy famously ridden by Arnold Schwarzenegger in 1991's hit flick *Terminator 2: Judgment Day*.

After Arnie's character arrives on Earth, he enters a biker bar, identifies a regular of similar build and promptly demands: 'I need your clothes, your boots and your motorcycle.' The rest, as they say, is history ...

The Fat Boy's creation was almost as dramatic. Following the success of Harley's 1984 Softail (which introduced both the 'Evolution' V-twin engine and 'Softail' rear suspension), then the 1986 Heritage Softail (which debuted 1950s balloon-tyre styling), Harley's designers, headed by company founder grandson Willie G. Davidson, were encouraged to be bolder still.

With co-designer Louie Netz, they did just that. Starting with the fussy concho-ed and chromed Heritage Softail, they aimed for a more minimal, industrial look. Although the base mechanicals were those of the Heritage, in being an 82-cubic-inch (1,340cc) air-cooled, pushrod V-twin held in the same tubular steel, 'Softail' frame, the styling and many of the parts were new – and as plain as possible. Striking, solid disc wheels replaced wires, twin 'shotgun' pipes were introduced, fork shrouds and fenders were pared back and the whole lot was given a monochromatic silver (or black) livery.

WHAT THEY SAID

'The Fat Boy is so outlandish it's sure to be a tremendous hit. In the best two-wheels-and-an-engine fashion, almost any Harley is a study in mechanical function, but the Fat Boy, with its alloy disc wheels, jumbo fenders and steel-silver paint, has taken that image a notch higher. It's a full-metal motorcycle.'

Cycle World, March 1990, on the $10,995 Fat Boy

The Fat Boy had been the brainchild of Harley styling chief Willie G. Davidson, went on to become a bestseller and remains a core bike in the brand's range even today. (Harley-Davidson)

WHO LOVED IT?

An instant bestseller, the Fat Boy also earned a place in American pop culture after appearances not just in *T:2* but numerous other shows. Arnie's bike is now on display at Harley's Museum in Milwaukee. The repeatedly updated Fat Boy lives on today as one of Harley's longest-lived and most-loved models.

The fat look inspired the name; PR prototype events followed in Daytona and Sturgis and, when launched in 1990, the Fat Boy became an instant bestseller – enough for Hollywood to take note, make it Arnie's ride and propel it to superstardom.

APRILIA AF1 FUTURA, 1990

One of the most beautiful sports bikes of the 1990s, the AF1 had it all – inverted forks,
single-sided swingarm and aluminium twin-beam frame – and yet was only a 125! (Aprilia)

If the early 1990s were golden years for hyperbikes and Harleys, they were incandescent ones for screaming racer-replica two-stroke 'learner' 125s.

And no nation did them better than Italy.

While the 'Big Four' Japanese flooded the market with junior GP replicas such as Yamaha's TZR125 and Suzuki's RG125, both attractive but affordable 'half-size' versions of bikes then dominating 250 production racing, the Italian brands were coming up with the most exotic, mouth-watering, highest performing and expensive 125s ever seen.

Cagiva launched its first Freccia 125 in 1987 followed by the astonishing seven-speed, 33bhp Mito in 1989 and its Supermoto sister, the mouth-watering Super City in 1992.

Gilera followed up its GP-alike 1990 SP02 with the simply space-age, hub-centre-steered CX125 in 1991.

But the most radical, highly specced and, arguably, best-performing 'learner' 125 of the early 1990s was from Aprilia.

The Noale-based brand had been rejuvenated in the late 1970s by Ivano Beggio and by the mid-1980s had the leading sports 125 with its AF1. With a 28+bhp, liquid-cooled, two-stroke single, aluminium beam frame, single-sided swingarm, inverted forks and GP styling it had it all – more, in fact, than most 750+cc sportsters.

WHAT THEY SAID

'I knifed through turns with more precision than ever before. The Sport Pro is classless. As good and as much fun as most 750s and beats the insurance vultures, too.'

Bike magazine, April 1992, on the £3,499 1992 Aprilia AF1 Sport Pro

The even more extreme (and powerful) Sport Production version was better still. Together they were among the ultimate 'poster bikes' for 1990s 17-year-olds. (Aprilia)

WHO LOVED IT?

While 17-year-old learners in the 1970s and early 1980s lusted after 250s such as Kawasaki's KH and Yamaha's LC, their 1990s equivalents made poster bikes of sports 125s. Most may have ended up with 'sensible' TZRs and ARs, but the AF1 (and Mito) were the ones they yearned for most.

But the best and most beautiful was the 1990 AF1 Futura, with 30bhp, and its even more extreme spin-off, the 1992, 33bhp AF1 Sport Pro. Yes, they were expensive, extreme and largely irrelevant for UK learners, who had to have them restricted. But they were also gorgeous, focused, fine-handling dream bikes for a whole generation; 125s had never been so desirable.

BIMOTA TESI 1D, 1990

With its radical hub-centre steering, fuel-injected Ducati 851 and digital dash, the Bimota Tesi 1D was one of the most advanced bikes of the 1990s – and looked like it could be from the 2020s. (Bimota)

With the onset of the 1990s Italian sporting exotica specialist Bimota needed a change of direction. With the 1990 Tesi 1D it got it – sort of.

After gaining success in the late 1970s and early 1980s on reframed, highly specced, fine-handling sportsters based on Japanese engines, by the end of the decade, thanks to the arrival of bikes like Honda's RC30 and Yamaha's FZR1000 EXUP, Bimotas were largely irrelevant.

WHAT THEY SAID

'It's been a long time coming, but the blueprint for the bike of the future is here. The Tesi streetbike should mark an important new stage in the evolution of the motorcycle. All that remains to be seen is how quickly the Japanese will seek to emulate it.'

Cycle World, May 1990, on the £25,000 Bimota Tesi 1D

So, instead of delivering merely 'fine handling', Bimota turned to hi-tech.

The pet project of Bimota chief engineer Pier Luigi Marconi, the Tesi was not only the world's first production bike with hub-centre steering, it was the first with a fully digital LED dash. Its engine was no longer a 'run-of-the-mill' Japanese transverse four, but Ducati's (hence the 'D') state-of-the-art desmodromic V-twin. Cycle parts were the best available from Marchesini, Brembo and Ohlins; bodywork was fully enclosed; its looks seemed like something from the future and so did, sadly, its price: £25,000 when a faster, better-handling EXUP could be had for a third of the cost.

WHO LOVED IT?

Just 127 851-powered examples were built during 1990–91, twenty more longer-stroke 1D 906s came in 1991–92 then 144 examples of the 1D SR in 1992–93. A further fifty 1D ES (Edizione Speciale) came in 1993, twenty-five 1D EFs (Edizione Finale) were built in 1994, while fifty-one examples of a special version for Japan were also built using the Ducati 400SS motor.

Unfortunately, the Tesi's hub-centre steering system, which relied on a series of rose-jointed connecting rods, proved flawed and vague. (Bimota)

First conceived by Martini for his engineering degree in the early 1980s ('Tesi' is Italian for 'Thesis'), the 1D had taken too long and cost too much to develop, almost bankrupting Bimota. And even when launched it proved flawed, with erratic steering and instruments, too much weight and a far too high price.

Bimota would bounce back, but the Tesi was never the success hoped for. It does, however, remain one of the most ambitious, striking and futuristic bikes ever built.

As a wonder of engineering and a simply glorious lump of metal, however, there was simply nothing else like it. (The front, by the way, is on the right.)(Bimota)

SUZUKI RGV250L, 1990

Suzuki's 'second-generation' RGV, the 1990 L, was a significant upgrade with 'banana' swingarm, 'Siamesed' exhausts, more power and even more stunning styling. (Suzuki)

For many of a certain age, the 1990 RGV250L is the ultimate incarnation of the favourite bike in the most compelling sports bike category of the 1990s – GP replica two-stroke 250s.

Although the RGV dates back to 1988, as the RGV250J, the V-twin successor to the RG250 parallel twin also designated the VJ21, that bike didn't officially come to the UK until 1989 as the RGV250K. And, with pure 250GP styling, a 90-degree, two-stroke V-twin fed by twin 32mm Mikuni carbs producing 57bhp, plus a beefy, twin spare aluminium frame, conventional 41mm telescopic forks and 17in front/18in rear wheel combo, there was no closer GP replica.

WHAT THEY SAID

'The RGV is at the stage of development where there is no room for anything other than perfection. You sometimes feel as if you've reached the RGV's limits, but the limits are your own.'

Performance Bikes magazine, May 1990, on the £3,599 RGV250L

Further subtle changes followed, including to the swingarm, but for a generation of two-stroke sportster fans in the early 1990s, the RGV250 was the ultimate. (Suzuki)

In truth, of course, there was: Japan's domestic 250 two-stroke/400cc four-stroke licence restriction had created a hugely popular 'supersports' class, but some of the most exotic offerings, such as Honda's NS and NSR250, were never officially exported to Britain, leading to the unofficial, 'grey import' of such bikes in the early 1990s.

But while the RGV-K was already good enough to dominate on track, in production racing and on the street, in 1990 it got better still. The RGV250L was a major update with a new electronic power valve (SAPC), digital ignition and larger 34mm carbs helping boost power to 59bhp, new 41mm inverted forks, a GP-alike 'banana' swingarm, bigger front discs, wider, 17in rear wheel and even racier styling. Just the thing, in fact, with which to mimic Suzuki GP god Kevin Schwantz.

Yes, there were other exotic 250s and the RGV itself arguably improved further until its demise in 1997, but, for most, the 1990 RGV250L was the ultimate.

WHO LOVED IT?

The choice of club racers, up-and-coming track stars (Jamie Whitham and Shakey Byrne among them), Schwantz and GP replica wannabes and street stroker headbangers everywhere. It's not recorded how many were sold, but most were crashed, stolen, raced, or all three, at some point.

With popular Texan Kevin Schwantz then riding high in grand prix racing aboard his factory Suzuki 500, the RGV was the perfect blank canvas for racer replica fans. (Suzuki)

KAWASAKI KR-1S, 1990

Early 1990s 'stroker' 250 sports-bike fans fell into one of two camps – for Suzuki's RGV or for Kawasaki's newly updated version of its KR-1, the KR-1S. (Kawasaki)

In the early 1990s world of two-stroke 250 GP replicas, if Suzuki's RGV250L was the maddest and most popular of the officially imported UK options, then Kawasaki's more subtle KR-1S ran it closest. Some connoisseur devotees, in fact, would say it was even better ...

Like Suzuki with the RGV250L, Kawasaki launched its predecessor, the KR-1, in 1988. But although plainer-looking and-specced than the Suzuki, with more slabby styling and a conventional, parallel twin, 55bhp engine, the Kawasaki compensated with calmer handling and sweeter steering.

Then, in 1990, Kawasaki moved things up a notch with the KR-1S. Although visually similar, the S boasted more power thanks to new exhausts and engine mods, a different frame, five (not three) spoke wheels and bigger brakes.

The biggest difference, though, was power – and speed. Producing 59.1bhp (against the Suzuki's 59 – that 0.1bhp was important), it was not only the most powerful 250 officially available, it was the fastest, too, recording over 139mph.

WHAT THEY SAID

'Like the RGV the KR-1S is a racer with lights. It'll be bought on the back of track success and fashion credentials and bugger everything else.'

Performance Bikes magazine, May 1990, on the £3,549 Kawasaki KR-1S

With more power, bigger brakes, wider tyres, a different frame and more, the S was a significant improvement over the old KR-1 and, crucially, *faster*. (Kawasaki)

On track there was little in it, with both the Kawasaki and Suzuki racking up countless Supersport 400 and Production 250 wins. On the street, each had its followers: headbanger race fans favoured the RGV, while less showy purists were happy tinkering with their KR-1S (the Kawasakis were notoriously unreliable). But for both, during those heady days of the early 1990s before the Kawasaki became the first to go 'off-sale' in 1992, those stroker twins were the best.

The KR-1S's exhausts, wheels and colour schemes were changed over the KR-1, too. (Kawasaki)

WHO LOVED IT?

The KR-1S may not have had the GP-alike glamour, Schwantz connotations and sexy tech of its Suzuki RGV rival, but it was faster in a straight line and something of a connoisseurs' choice. Some 5,800 examples of the preceding KR-1 were made, followed by 4,200 KR-1Ss.

HONDA VFR400R, 1990

Honda's VFR400R of 1990 was not only an exquisite V4 mini sports bike in its own right, it was the highlight of a whole new era of 400cc supersports. (Honda)

The hugely competitive supersports 400 category of the late 1980s/early 1990s, which primarily came about due to licensing regulations in Japan, resulted in a raft of 250cc two-stroke twins battling 400cc four-stroke fours, both on road and track.

The 'stroker' scene was dominated by Suzuki's RGV250 and Kawasaki's KR-1S, supplemented by even more exotic 'grey imports' from Japan, like Honda's NSR and Yamaha's TZR, all taking their cues from GP 250s.

Look familiar? The VFR400R was the Japanese market, 400cc 'little brother' to Honda's stupendous, world-beating, homologation special VFR750R/RC30 production racer. (Honda)

WHAT THEY SAID

'The VFR is a junior RC30: tiny, plush, immensely sophisticated – but toy like. A mini Rolls-Royce for mini oil sheikhs, a 400cc gag bike.'

Bike magazine, April 1991, on the £5,899 Honda VFR400R

But the latter four-stroke class was arguably even more exotic and spawned delectable, 'mini', 400cc versions of 750 superbikes such as Kawasaki's ZXR400 and Suzuki's GSX-R400, of which Honda's junior VFR750R/RC30 production racer was king.

Originally launched in 1989, a year after its bigger brother, the VFR400R (or NC30 as it was more popularly known) may have been a 'mini RC30' in looks and most respects but was actually a successor to the Japan-only 1988 NC24 and 1986 NC21, which were both more VFR750F-influenced.

It didn't matter. Although also 'Japan-only' in 1989, the NC30 was effectively an RC30 for the masses: it looked fabulous, handled impeccably and had the same droning, flexible V4 producing 59bhp. From 1990 it also became one of the few 400 officially available in the UK, instantly making it the dream bike of a generation, even if a price of £5,899 (more than both Hondas, CBR600F and VFR750F) kept it exclusive.

And although Honda's later 'baby Blade' CBR400RR and 1994 'mini RC45' RVF400R were arguably better (but not brought to the UK) and Yamaha's 1991 FZR400RR SP was faster, the NC30, fuelled by a steady flow of more affordable 'grey-import' examples, remained the definitive example of the breed.

WHO LOVED IT?

Everyone worshipped the RC30, but virtually no one could afford it, so the 'grey-import' NC30 was the affordable next best thing, a dream first big bike and the go-to replica for TT and world endurance wannabes.

YAMAHA FZR400RR SP, 1991

But the fastest and arguably most desirable of all the early 1990s Japanese import Supersport 400 machines was Yamaha's ballistically fast and beautifully handling FZR400RR SP. (Yamaha)

If Honda's 'mini RC30', the VFR400R/NC30, was the early 1990s supersports 400 for the masses, then the ultra-exclusive, uber-focused and eye-wateringly expensive Yamaha FZR400RR SP, which arrived shortly after, was the Supersport 400 for the gods.

Like the Honda V4 and nearly all its rivals, the little FZR was a development of earlier, Japan-only 400s dating back to the FZR400 of 1986, which evolved into the 60bhp 1988 FZR400R, then the 66bhp 1990 FZR400RR.

Japan's F3 racing series was proving successful at promoting the breed domestically so most manufacturers also produced limited-edition, tuned, homologation versions, with the first FZR400R SP (for Sport Production),

The SP Sport Production was a more extreme, more powerful derivative of the preceding FZR400RR. (Yamaha)

emerging in 1989. But the ultimate was the 1991 FZR400RR SP, a 'mini-OW-01' in all but name with a screaming 66bhp at 12,500rpm, single race seat, multi-adjustable suspension and exquisite handling.

It wasn't alone, of course. Honda, Kawasaki and Suzuki all offered 'pocket rockets', too. But the Yamaha was the most powerful, focused, sharpest handling and hardest braking. After the FZR, the VFR400R felt like a soft all-rounder.

WHAT THEY SAID

'It's very hard to write about the FZR400RR SP's qualities: braking, acceleration, flexibility, build quality, stability – just think of a cliché and double it. For steering and suspension think of a cliché and treble it.'

Bike magazine, May 1991, on the £6,436 Yamaha FZR400RR SP

Along with improved, multi-adjustable suspension, reduced weight and a single race seat, the SP version also got more power, making it the most potent 400 Supersports available. (Yamaha)

As a result, the FZR became the racers' choice. At the 1991 TT, Dave Leach won the Supersport 400 race, with Yamahas filling six of the top seven places.

It was also enough to convince Yamaha to, briefly, officially import it into the UK at the heady price of £6,436. It wasn't cheap – the best never are – but for a brief, brilliant moment, the FZR400RR SP was the most delectable 400 of all.

WHO LOVED IT?

A 'mini OW-01' in specification, performance, handling and price, the FZR400RR SP also aped its bigger brother in terms of exclusivity – just 100 were officially imported into the UK, almost all destined for the track.

CAGIVA MITO 125, 1991

Aprilia didn't quite have everything its own way in the quarter-litre class in the early 1990s. Italian compatriot Cagiva had the equally tempting Mito 125, especially as here in 1993 'Lawson Replica' form. (Cagiva)

In the early 1990s, the exquisite Cagiva Mito 125 was to its great Italian 125cc sportster rival, the Aprilia AF1, what Kawasaki's KR-1S was to Suzuki's RGV in the quarter-litre class – its only serious rival.

Where the AF1, like the RGV250, had all the latest, sexy sporting developments – inverted forks, a hi-tech swingarm and so on – the blood-red Mito, which had first been launched in 1989 but reached its zenith with the 1991/92 'Lawson Replica', responded with an utterly uncompromising raw focus.

Tech, refinement and versatility wise, the Mito couldn't match the 'Priller. Its forks were conventional, its mirrors useless, the gearbox notchy, but it didn't really matter. It made up for it in spades with a peak power output of 33.5bhp (a touch more than the AF1, even in Sport Pro guise), a paper-thin powerband that required a seven-speed gearbox, a gossamer-light weight of just 125kg WET,

WHAT THEY SAID

'Every moment has to be invested in keeping the engine singing around its power peak. Achieve that and the Mito is a ball. Fail, and you'd get more fun out of a moped.'

Performance Bikes, June 1991, on the £3,499 Cagiva Mito

Initially a razor-edged 125cc sportsbike with its own style, later versions of the Mito were modified to make it more resemble a 'mini Ducati 916' (Cagiva at that time also owned Ducati). (Cagiva)

ultra-sharp steering even the Aprilia couldn't match and, naturally, Cagiva 500 GP replica styling now complete with Eddie Lawson No. 7 race number and team decals.

Aprilia's AF1 may have been more sophisticated, more rounded, better developed and overall a better bike, but the Mito was the ultimate 1990s 125 if owning a credible, convincing GP replica was your goal.

WHO LOVED IT?

As with the RGV/KR-1S rivalry in the 250 class, in 125s you were either in the Aprilia or Cagiva camp. The Aprilia was slicker with a better UK dealer network, but the Cagiva was sharper, faster, a mini 500GP bike – and had seven gears!

YAMAHA FZR1000RU EXUP, 1991

The last of the 'old-school' heavyweight superbikes rendered obsolete by Honda's lightweight FireBlade, the 1991 Yamaha FZR1000RU EXUP was also the best – and most beautiful. (Yamaha)

If early 1990s motorcycling was characterised most by the sea-change shift in large-capacity sports bikes, from heavyweights such as Suzuki's GSX-R1100 to a new breed of compact lightweights initiated by Honda's game-changing 1992 CBR900RR FireBlade, then Yamaha's 'second generation' FZR1000RU EXUP of 1991 was surely the ultimate example of the old guard.

Originally launched as the FZR1000R EXUP in 1989, itself an upgrade on the 1987 FZR1000 Genesis, in 1991 the EXUP was honed even further with new inverted front forks and sharper styling, with a new, single headlight front cowling.

Those improvements may have seemed minor but you have to remember the brilliant base bike it was built on. The 1987 999cc Genesis redefined litre-class superbikes by being the first fully integrated design complete with a five-valve head, 135bhp and GP-alike, aluminium, twin-spar 'Deltabox' frame. The

WHAT THEY SAID

'This is a sportbike like no other, one that leaves even inveterate speed junkies slack-jawed and searching for superlatives. For the past four years, the FZR 1000 has defined the cutting edge of large-displacement sportbikes. The edge just got sharper.'

Cycle World, April 1991, on the $8,749 Yamaha FZR1000RU

Among the key updates for the RU version was the adoption (like most sports bikes of this era) of new, more rigid 'upside-down' or inverted telescopic front forks. (Yamaha)

There was also a new headlight and subtle other changes, but at its heart, the FZR, with its Deltabox II frame and EXUP-equipped, five-valve, four-cylinder, 1,003cc engine, was unchanged. (Yamaha)

WHO LOVED IT?

Between 1989 and 1992 the EXUP, no matter what some Suzuki GSX-R1100 fans might say, was king of the superbikes – fast, fine handling, classy and beautiful. The RU was the ultimate incarnation of the breed.

EXUP in 1989 added power-boosting electronic exhaust valves that, along with three extra cc, boosted power to 145bhp, while, on top of that, gaining a revised, more rigid 'Deltabox II' frame with sharper steering and better-looking bodywork.

It was all enough for the 1989 model to be crowned 'Bike of the Decade' by some critics, leaving, you would think, nowhere for any improved version to go. The 1991 RU achieved just that.

Sure, its reign, due to the imminent 1992 FireBlade, was short, while a further, final 'Foxeye' facelift in 1994 was largely irrelevant, but in 1991 the FZR1000RU EXUP was as good as superbikes got.

DUCATI 888, 1990-93

Massimo Bordi's original liquid-cooled 851 had revolutionised Ducati but the Italian firm's flagship superbike reached its zenith in 888 form and particularly in top-spec SP trim. (Ducati)

Although Ducati's revolutionary 851, with Massimo Bordi's all-new 'Desmoquattro', the four-valve, liquid-cooled, modernisation of the Bologna brand's traditional 90-degree 'L-twin' with desmodromically actuated valves, debuted in 1987, it only truly came 'on song', both on road and track, when updated to 888cc from 1990.

That year saw the release of the 851 SP2 homologation special, which had an engine

WHAT THEY SAID

'The deceptive 888 ate up the turns on Willow Springs' hard and fast corners. The result was a scorching 1:34 lap that left the Honda and Yamaha gasping in awe. The 888 outperformed both class winners on the street, too. It didn't look especially quick, it didn't feel fast and that lagging tachometer lied about the rpm, but the 888 with its superior grip and unlimited lean angle outpaced the opposition.'

Motor Cyclist magazine, July 1991, on the $20,400 Ducati 851 SP2

On track in WSB, the 851 and 888 were proving to be *the* bikes to have and paved the way for the later dominance of Ducati's subsequent 916. This is Doug Polen. (Ducati)

The full-race-spec 'Corsa' versions, complete with Ohlins suspension, Marchesini wheels, slicks and even more power were 'out-of-the-crate' racers. (Ducati)

with a 2mm larger 94mm bore, taking capacity to 888cc, and was the bike that formed the basis of the machine factory rider Raymond Roche rode to Ducati's first World Superbike Championship.

This was then succeeded by the 1991 SP3, distinguished by louder and higher Termignoni exhausts, black Brembo wheels and higher compression pistons, which, with a forced air intake, boosted power to 118bhp. That year Doug Polen claimed the WSB for Ducati.

In 1992, it was updated again, called the 888 SP4 (with an even more exotic SPS version offered) and gained further updates including a swoopier seat unit, with Polen again winning the world crown.

The final year of the 851/888 was to be 1993, with the SP5 the ultimate incarnation, but by then it was largely irrelevant. The Desmoquattro/851 had come good; the point had been proven and the succeeding 916 was just around the corner ...

WHO LOVED IT?

The first truly competitive Ducati superbike in a generation, the 888 was the dream bike not only of Italophiles but also connoisseurs of its next-generation V-twin tech. The SPs, meanwhile, instantly became the production superbike racer of choice. A total of 7,591 examples of all types were built up to 1994.

KAWASAKI ZXR400, 1991

Kawasaki's take on the Supersports 400 theme, the ZXR400m, was effectively a 'mini ZXR750J' and shared its big brother's howling, rev-hungry four and sweet-steering front end. (Kawasaki)

If Honda's 'mini-RC30', the 1990 VFR400R, had been the most exotic of the hugely popular, early 1990s supersports 400s, while Yamaha's more extreme FZR400RR SP had been the fastest and most successful on track, then Kawasaki's second-generation 1991 ZXR400 was surely the '400 for the people'.

Like most of its Japanese rivals, by the 1990s Kawasaki had produced four-cylinder sports 400s for the hugely competitive domestic market for years, first with the 1985 GPz400R, then the 1988 ZX-4. But the first ZXR, with 'R' denoting racer Replica, didn't come until 1989 as effectively a mini-version of the ZXR750H1. That bike, however, unlike its bigger brother, was never officially imported to the UK.

But when the 'second-generation' ZXR750, the swoopy J1, arrived in Blighty in 1991, it was accompanied by its junior sibling. And, with a howling 59bhp at 12,000rpm, one of the best front ends in biking and a price of 'just' £4,799 compared to £6,436 for the Yam, it became the most popular of all.

Although less extreme and sophisticated than homologation specials such as Yamaha's FZR400RR SP, and therefore not as competitive on track, the ZXR was a great 400 'for the people'. (Kawasaki)

On the road it was the most affordable and arguably intoxicating four-cylinder mini superbike of all. In plain blue or Kawasaki green tricolour it looked fantastic. Its revvy powerplant gave the soundtrack to match and, like its 750 big brother, it had one of the best-steering, best-braking front ends anywhere. Even if it didn't have quite the ultimate speed and exotic appeal of its Yamaha and Honda rivals, it was a true mini superbike for the masses.

WHAT THEY SAID

'The noise experience is total – pained but the best. Initially I changed up too early. I couldn't believe it could wail so without blowing up. Soon after I was addicted. This 400cc interpretation of ZXR performance is safe, fun, unintimidating and intense.'

Bike magazine, August 1991, on the £4,799 Kawasaki ZXR400

WHO LOVED IT?

Forget the 'grey-import' VFR400Rs or ultra-exclusive FZR400RR SPs, the mass-market, comparatively affordable, howlingly fast ZXR400 was the four-stroke 400cc super-sports for the common man.

Unlike most, the ZXR400 was officially imported into the UK from 1991, more affordable than most rivals and so also made a great 'first big' bike and initiation into four-cylinder sports bikes. (Kawasaki)

HONDA CBR600F2, 1991

Honda's first CBR600F in 1987 had been a huge success, cementing the popularity of the supersports 600 category. Its second in 1991, the CBR600F2, was better in every way. (Honda)

If one motorcycle could be said to sum up the whole of the 1990s, it was surely Honda's second-generation CBR6 – the F2.

Launched in 1991 as an all-new successor to the original 1987 'jelly mould' CBR600F, the F2 arrived at the right time. Kawasaki had briefly snatched the category crown with its fast but big ZZ-R600 in what was by then already the most competitive class of all, while Yamaha was constantly updating its head-banging racer favourite, the FZR600. Honda's challenge, then, was to come up with a 600 that was both sufficiently sporty to win on track yet also continue to be the consummate, affordable all-rounder for the road.

It achieved exactly that – and more.

Its new, swoopy bodywork was subtly beautiful; power from the uprated 598cc four rose from 85bhp to 100 (more than both the 98bhp Kawa and 91bhp Yam); its ergonomics, in typical Honda fashion, were sportily spot on; and, although its box-section steel frame was a little basic and budget, its handling dynamics were more than a match and, looks wise, it didn't matter as it was hidden away.

Fast, fine-handling and affordable, all-enclosing bodywork helped cut costs (negating the need for a 'cosmetic' frame and engine) and the result was one of the best-selling bikes of the decade. (Honda)

WHAT THEY SAID

'Comfortable ergonomics, agile handling and more horsepower than anything else in the class make the CBR600F2 the machine to beat.'

Motor Cyclist magazine, June 1991, on the $4,998 Honda CBR600F2

Opposite: Further, more subtle updates came in 1995 with ram air intakes, revised bodywork, bigger brakes and improved cartridge front forks. This F3 version remains arguably the best CBR-F of all. (Honda)

WHO LOVED IT?

Honda's CBR600F, in all guises, was arguably the definitive all-round motorcycle of the late 1980s and early to mid-1990s. Consistently the best (and best-selling) supersport 600, it's estimated that more than 50,000 were sold between 1987 and 1993.

The result was classy, comfortable, fast, practical and affordable – so much so that it was an instant bestseller on the street and a repeated winner on track. It remained so – thus becoming the definitive supersports 600 – even with a 1995 update (bigger discs, ram air and styling tweaks), until finally usurped by Yamaha's radical R6 in 1999. No 1990s bike sold better or defined the decade so well.

YAMAHA FZR600, 1991

In the early 1990s, the supersport 600 class was the most popular and competitive of all. Yamaha's offering, the FZR600, was sporty and great on track but couldn't match the new CBR's versatility. (Yamaha)

Of all the hugely popular early 1990s supersports 600s, the purest, most track-focused, most manic was surely Yamaha's 'mini Genesis', the FZR600.

Launched in 1989 as a junior version of the FZR1000 EXUP, the 599cc interpretation shared its big brother's twin headlight styling and Deltabox (albeit steel instead of aluminium) frame and, with 90bhp from its four-valve, four-cylinder engine and lightest-in-class 179kg dry weight, instantly became *the* choice of supersports racers everywhere.

WHAT THEY SAID

'If you want a bike for all reasons, get a CBR or GPX or GSX. If you want something more frantically focused, the FZR's the one for you. Just don't blame us when your pillion gives you a hard time.'

Performance Bikes magazine, September 1991, on the £5,299 FZR600

Previously updated in 1989, the FZR mimicked its 1,000cc big brother but with a steel frame, four-valve engine and twin piston brakes and, up to the arrival of the CBR F2 in 1991, dominated on track. (Yamaha)

In 1990 it swept the first five places in the TT Supersport race. But the updated 1991 version was better still. Like the 1000, it gained a new, single-lens headlight, improved four-piston brake calipers and wider rear tyre; enough, in fact, despite the arrival of Honda's new CBR600F2, for the FZR to remain the racer and scratcher's bike of choice. It won the British Supersport 600 championship that year in the hands of Ian Simpson.

It didn't last, admittedly – a further update came in 1994 when it became the FZR600R, gained new 'foxeye' styling, frame and more, but by then its time in the spotlight, like that of the FZR1000RU, was over.

However, that doesn't diminish its significance either: for the first few years of the 1990s, the FZR600 was the sharpest, most nimble and sportiest 600 of all and the supersports 600 track king.

1991 saw a new single-headlight fairing and new four-piston brake calipers but, although an improvement and still a great, sporty bike, it wasn't enough to keep the Honda at bay. (Yamaha)

WHO LOVED IT?

Although the 1991 model was the best FZR yet, in truth, with the arrival of Honda's CBR600F2, its star was already on the wane. In 1990 the FZR had swept the top five at the TT; in 1991 it was Honda's turn. Even so, the Yamaha remained loved for being the sportiest of the 600s.

KAWASAKI ZXR750J1, 1991

Kawasaki's first ZXR750, the 1989 H1, had been a true racer replica for the street. But the succeeding 1991 ZXR750J1, although no faster, was sweeter, more stylish and became one of the iconic bikes of the 1990s. (Kawasaki)

If Kawasaki's first ZXR750, the H1 of 1989, was an endurance-inspired racer replica intended for the working man, then its successor, the 1991 ZXR750J1, then the 1993 ZXR750L1, took things to another level on the road and, in homologation race spec as the ZXR750K and M respectively, on track.

With new, more curvy and aggressive styling, plus the lairy early 1990s colour schemes to match, the J also boasted new inverted forks, a lighter, diamond-section beam frame, new short-stroke engine and yet still cost just £6,379 (when an RC30 cost 10 grand).

Admittedly, its 100bhp peak power was 5bhp down on the H (due to concerns over a proposed new European power limit) and early examples' rear shocks were rock hard, but it didn't matter: the ZXR-J looked great, had one of the best front ends around (again) and, with race wins across the globe (Doug Chandler, then Scott Russell won AMA titles, Kawasaki France dominated world endurance, most famously with Brits Carl Fogarty and Terry Rymer in 1992, the same year that John Reynolds won the British championship for Team Green, while Russell went on to claim the 1993 WSB crown in 1993), it became the 'poster bike' 750 of the day.

The 1991 J was updated into the 1993 ZXR750L with more power due to a revised ram air system, updated nose to suit and improved geometry and suspension. The style, however, was unchanged. (Kawasaki)

WHAT THEY SAID

'It's still my bike of the year, even if seven grand doesn't buy you a real-roads shock. Riding the J home in fog and stop-go traffic I was in top gear, lazily rolling the tach needle around it midrange, nipping past a lorry here, a gaggle of Sierras there ... I was riding a J and, together we were doing very nicely, thank you.'

Bike magazine, August 1991,
on the £6,379 Kawasaki ZXR750J1

Kawasaki also produced limited production 'homologation special' race-kitted versions – the 1991 ZXR750K and, here, the 1993 ZXR750M/R with race seat, flat-slide carbs and more. (Kawasaki)

It was also a survivor long after its peak glory days on track and street dominance (after the arrival of Honda's FireBlade in 1992) were long gone. The 1993 L got a ram air nose and 18 extra bhp, then in 1996 it morphed into the ZX-7R, as which it continued as one of the most recognisable racer replicas of all, right into the new millennium.

WHO LOVED IT?

With the RC30 prohibitively expensive and Suzuki's GSX-R750 ageing and old fashioned, the fast, affordable and fabulous-looking ZXR was *the* 750 superbike racer replica for the man in the street – especially in green.

2

BOLD NEW BREEDS

The 1990s also saw experimentation in bike design ranging from Honda's oval-pistoned NR750 to Yamaha's hub-centre-steered GTS1000. Ducati's parts-bin naked roadster, the Monster, was one of the most successful. (Ducati)

HONDA NR750, 1992

The astonishing NR750 was nothing more than a Honda showcase of its corporate craft with oval pistons, under-seat exhausts, carbon-fibre bodywork, titanium-coated screen and more. (Honda)

It's no overstatement to say that, in 1992, Honda unveiled the most extravagant, technically advanced, most ambitious motorcycle ever built: the NR750.

And yet, actually, it wasn't very good. It wasn't the fastest. It wasn't the lightest. It wasn't very practical. But the NR remains, to this day, probably the most ambitious, sophisticated and arguably desirable two-wheeler ever put into production.

What set the NR apart was its revolutionary 'oval-pistoned' V4 engine. Built after Honda's ultra-ambitious NR500 GP then NR750 endurance-racing projects were finally canned (where Honda sought, but failed, to beat rival 500cc two-strokes with a novel and complex four-cylinder, four-stroke that mimicked the combustion of a V8 via its unique piston design), the road-going NR was Honda's corporate two fingers to all those who doubted it. The NR750 was never intended to sell in numbers. Each cost £36,000. Today they're worth more than double.

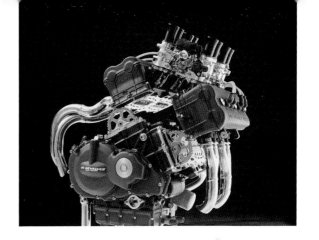

Top right: The NR's engine was the star. Derived from Honda's failed 500GP project, it was a four-stroke V4 that attempted to match the power of a two-stroke (despite having half as many power strokes). (Honda)

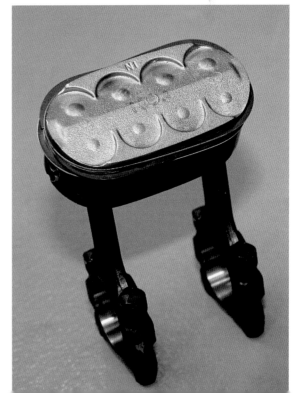

Bottom right: To do that, within the constraints of a four-cylinder limit, the NR was effectively a V8 with thirty-two valves but with pairs of pistons merged into 'oval' pistons each with twin conrods. (Honda)

WHAT THEY SAID

'The NR is an art piece, a Faberge Egg of a motorcycle, destined more to a life of collecting dust than stone chips on its belly pan. For fans of high-performance, high-tech hardware, the 32-valve, oval piston NR truly is the Holy Grail on Michelin TX radials.'

Cycle World magazine, August 1994, on the $60,000 NR750

Even the NR's dash was exotic – a carbon-fibre panel with conventional oil temperature, water temperature and central tacho dials placed beneath a pioneering LED digital speedo. (Honda)

The eight-valve engine was just the start. The NR also boasted pioneering fuel injection; the first LCD dash; the first under-seat exhausts and a single-sided swingarm (both being copied on the Ducati 916); carbon-fibre bodywork; and even a titanium-coated screen.

On the downside, its 125bhp was adequate rather than exceptional, its 160mph top speed nothing special and its 223kg dry weight on the porky side, but when a bike's as good-looking and extravagant as the NR, who cares?

WHO LOVED IT?

So extreme, expensive and precious even Honda never seriously expected anyone to buy the NR, let alone ride one on the street. Instead, it became an instant collectable for a few ultra-wealthy afficionados – just 322 were built.

HONDA CBR900RR FIREBLADE, 1992

Its understated black alternative colour scheme may have been less dramatic than the most popular red, white and blue option but that takes nothing away from the significance of the 1992 Honda CBR900RR FireBlade. (Honda)

The FireBlade was not just the most significant sports bike of the 1990s, it was arguably the most influential motorcycle of the last quarter of the twentieth century.

Not bad for a bike that, really, contained no revolutionary technology, wasn't the fastest or most powerful and was also a Honda that, let's face it, by 1992, homologation special RC30 aside, hadn't produced a pure, big-bore sports bike for a decade.

The FireBlade changed all that.

The brainchild of engineer Tadao Baba, the FireBlade's brilliance was in having the power and performance of a 1,000cc superbike but with the more manageable weight and dimensions of a 600. (Honda)

Extreme measures were taken by Baba and his team to keep the original 'Blade's weight as low as possible. Note, for example, the holes in the fairing by the headlight and in the 'belly pan'. (Honda)

WHAT THEY SAID

'If you want the quickest A–B road bike around, this is it. No contest. What it also is for me, however, is the most exhilarating, sexiest sports bike around by a country mile; a much more forgiving, more practical day to day bike than you could possibly imagine and, possibly, THE bike I want more than any other.'

Bike magazine, May 1992, on the £7,390 Honda CBR900RR FireBlade

It was the pet project of design engineer Tadao Baba, who later recalled: 'It was in 1989 and I was riding with a group of Honda engineers on some competitor machines, a Suzuki GSX-R1100, Yamaha FZR1000 and our own CBR1000F. I was thinking, "How can these be called sports bikes when they are so very big and heavy?" They didn't deserve the name.'

In response Baba began developing a new sports motorcycle concept with the working title 'Total Control' whereby the overriding principle was to create a larger-capacity sports machine that was both fun to ride and easy to control.

The first result was a prototype lightweight and compact 750 sportster dubbed the CBR750RR. But as Honda already had the V4 VFR750F and production racer VFR750R (RC30), a larger version was suggested. This time, a 1,000cc machine was ruled out as Honda already had the CBR1000F. Instead, Baba proposed retaining the dimensions of the 750 but increasing the motor's stroke to boost capacity to 893cc. The result, the CBR900RR FireBlade, at just 1.8kg heavier than Honda's CBR600F2 but with litre-class capacity, was effectively the size of a 600 but with the performance of a 1000.

It was even more radical to ride – manageable, unintimidating, even docile at low speed, the 'Blade was simply ballistic, explosive, dynamic and yet nimble with its throttle wide open – so much so, in fact, that with its quick-steering 16in front wheel, some feared it was too flighty.

It wasn't. On the road, despite 'only' 118bhp, the 'Blade blitzed everything. It might not have had any radical technology but its fastidious weight saving took rivals years to replicate. The successively updated 'Blade was only finally usurped in 1998 by Yamaha's all-new R1.

Instead, the 'Blade's only failing was on track, where, TT apart, it never had any significant success. As a 900 it neither qualified for the 750cc superbike formula nor had the power to match lightened 1,000+cc racers. Still, you can't have everything ...

The second-generation FireBlade from 1994 had revised 'foxeye' headlights and the option of a popular 'Urban Tiger' colour scheme. (Honda)

WHO LOVED IT?

The FireBlade was so revolutionary it turned the superbike class on its head. Previous Yamaha and Suzuki owners bought a Honda for the first time and, although never relevant on track, it became the benchmark sports bike for the next six years.

GILERA NORDWEST, 1992

The first production 'supermoto', the Gilera Nordwest, was based around a punchy, 600cc, single-cylinder enduro bike but with street suspension, wheels, brakes, tyres and headlamp fairing. (Gilera)

Supermotos – motocross-derived, performance singles modified for the street – may today seem to have been around for years, but in the 1990s the first production example of these hedonistic hooligan machines caused a sensation: the Gilera Nordwest 600.

The supermoto had been conceived in the late 1970s, when the US Superbikers series saw dirt- and road-race stars race adapted MX-ers on dual-surface circuits for TV cash prizes.

From there, DIY-built bikes gained a niche following before Italian manufacturer Gilera boldly decided to test the waters with a production version.

It didn't do it by halves. The Nordwest not only boasted a liquid-cooled, four-valve single producing nearly 50bhp, there was top-notch inverted Marzocchi forks, twin front discs with Grimeca four-piston calipers, lightweight cast wheels and slinky bodywork.

WHAT THEY SAID

'At £4500 it is a bit pricey and it is also in an unusual bracket but the bark of the Nordwest, the satisfying grunt, the sweet handling and rarity value make up for a lot. On balance I'd say it was just about worth it.'

Performance Bikes magazine, February 1992, on the £4,595 Gilera Nordwest

Although never a big seller due to its price, limited practicality and restricted availability, the Nordwest paved the way for all 'supermotos' that followed. (Gilera)

It was as light, punchy and lively as that sounds, too – but with an upright manageability that tempted you to carve up city traffic. In 1992 there were few other ways to have as much fun up to 50mph.

Unfortunately, however, the Nordwest was also as expensive as all that sounds and as practical as a chocolate teapot, so hardly anyone bought one. But we all secretly wished we had ...

WHO LOVED IT?

Although alluring, entertaining and exotic, the Nordwest was also expensive, impractical and rare, meaning few made it on to UK roads despite remaining in limited production up to 1994. Few survive today.

YAMAHA GTS1000, 1993

Although by 1993 radical steering and front-suspension alternatives to traditional telescopic forks were nothing new – Bimota debuted its hub-centre-steered Tesi two years earlier, while Elf-Honda had long been racing its GP version – none had been a conspicuous success nor put into mass production ... until Yamaha's GTS1000.

WHAT THEY SAID

'The GTS is a joy. Once you're familiar with its length and weight it's a doddle to ride fast and smooth. Stability is immense, the weight, carried low, gives Weeble-like properties, and the steering, with geometry tighter than an EXUP's, is light and accurate.'

Bike magazine, March 1993, on the £9,999 Yamaha GTS1000

Co-developed with Californian James Parker and based on a detuned FZR1000 EXUP powertrain, the GTS was intended to be Yamaha's new sports-touring flagship that reasserted its technical credentials and shook up the conventionally suspended establishment.

Far more sophisticated than the Bimota system, the Yamaha's unique hub-centre steering system was co-developed with Californian James Parker of RADD Design. (Yamaha)

Like other bold Yamaha experiments since – the MT-01 and VMAX spring to mind – it was only a partial success. Although the hub-centre front gave immense stability and impressively accurate steering, the GTS's hefty weight (and length) also made it cumbersome. Its detuned 100bhp engine – although smooth, a fuel injection pioneer and fast at 140mph – lacked the flexibility and shaft drive of some rivals, while its smooth fairing wasn't as protective (or pretty) as some. Worst of all, at £9,999, the GTS was prohibitively expensive.

As a result, sales of the radical, unproven Yamaha, in a conservative market sector then dominated by the sensible Honda ST1100 Pan European and BMW's K-series, were slow. Yamaha persevered until it was quietly discontinued after four years. And while the GTS's commercial failure ensured the continuing dominance of telescopic forks, the memory of it is of a bold new vision that broke the mould, if not motorcyclists' buying habits. If it had succeeded who knows what we might have been riding today ...

Its 'Omega Frame Concept' used swingarms front and rear. The engine, meanwhile, was a detuned version of the FZR1000 EXUP's four-cylinder unit. (Yamaha)

WHO LOVED IT?

Although able, the GTS was considered too expensive and unusual to be a sales
success. In the US it was only sold for a year and production was abandoned in 1997.
Today, however, it's increasingly viewed as an appreciating if oddball classic.

BMW R1100RS, 1993

Another manufacturer experimenting with
technology in the early 1990s was BMW.
Its all-new 1993 R1100RS not only had a
brand-new, oil-cooled boxer engine, but also
novel 'Telelever' front suspension. (BMW)

In the early 1990s this historic German brand was about to undertake a transformation bigger than any since its first bike, the R32, in 1923.

By the late 1970s the Bavarian marque had become reliant, almost to the point of bankruptcy, on a succession of touring-orientated, air-cooled boxer twins that had become increasingly expensive and uncompetitive in the face of a new breed of Japanese superbikes. Disaster was avoided when the surprise success of its quickly developed first 'adventure' bike, the 1980 R80G/S, gave BMW the breathing space needed

After the not wholly successful K-series, BMW reinvented its traditional, popular, boxer twin powertrain with oil cooling, extra cubes and more power. The R1100RS was its first recipient. (BMW)

WHAT THEY SAID

'The bike that most successfully combines performance and comfort is BMW's beautiful new R1100RS. R should stand for Renaissance because that's how this bike feels compared to the last boxer: reborn.'

Cycle World, August 1993, on the $13,656 BMW R1100RS

to develop its all-new, liquid-cooled K-series, launched in 1983. But by the late 1980s it was also clear that BMW's traditional buyers weren't convinced by the K and that an all-new, modern boxer twin was required. The 1993 R1100RS was the result, and a revelation, and would pave the way for an all-new dynasty of BMWs.

The R1100RS's chassis was equally radical with both front and rear suspension bolted to the engine (the front being the novel 'Telelever' design) and having small subframes for the seat and steering. (BMW)

The R1100RS was a revelation, not just because its engine was new – but because *everything* was new. The motor, code-named R259, although a shaft-drive boxer twin, now had oil-cooled heads, fuel injection and produced a competitive 90bhp. Rather than a conventional frame, front and rear subframes hung off the motor, and instead of conventional telescopic forks, it had BMW's novel 'Telelever' system. The list went on.

The K-series, highlighted by radical bikes such as the K1, deserved credit for getting the whole 'innovative BMW motorrad' ball rolling. But the new boxer cemented its route to success. After the R1100RS motorcyclists wouldn't think of BMW in the staid old way again ...

The resulting machine, the 1993 R1100RS sports tourer, completely modernised BMW and paved the way for a succession of spin-off boxer models, including the R1100GS, R1100R and R1100RT. (BMW)

WHO LOVED IT?

After the unconvincing K-series, the R1100 was the truly modern boxer BMW fans had been waiting for and paved the way for the even bigger-selling R1100GS and R1100RT that formed the foundation for the resurgent German marque.

DUCATI M900 MONSTER, 1993

It might look familiar today but back in 1993 Ducati's naked roadster, the Monster 900, was a revelation and was such a sales hit it spawned a whole family that lives on to this day. (Ducati)

Everyone thinks it was Ducati's 1994 916 superbike that revitalised the Italian marque in the 1990s and set it on a path to sustained success. To a degree, they're right: the 916's global plaudits re-established Ducati among the exotica elite and its track success, largely in the hands of Brit Carl Fogarty, re-established it as a proven winner.

But it was the preceding year's M900 Monster that, commercially, was far more significant, with huge sales helping finance Bologna's rebirth and whose style, fun factor and accessibility fuelled the growth of a whole new class – super nakeds.

Its creation was also something of a fluke. Conceived by junior, up-and-coming Cagiva (who then owned Ducati) designer Miguel Galluzzi, who'd been inspired by the crash-damaged Californian canyon racers he'd ridden in his youth, and created largely in secret and in his spare time, it was a 'parts-bin special' assembled out of fairly random Ducati components.

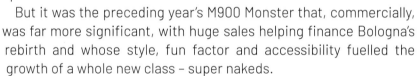

The Monster was the brainchild of up-and-coming Argentine designer Miguel Galluzzi, who today heads up Piaggio's Design Centre in Pasadena, California. (Ducati)

The air-cooled V-twin was from the 900SS, its frame with rising rate rear suspension from the 851, while its forks and brakes were taken from the smaller 750SS. The result, with a bespoke, almost phallic tank, straight bars and minimal, single-dial clocks, was striking to look at; an easy, characterful and hilarious, wheelie-prone hoon to ride and, when it arrived in the shops, a temptingly affordable (for a Ducati) £7,200 to buy.

WHAT THEY SAID

'This is probably the most distinctive, startling and crowd-pulling bike of recent times. That it's also a Ducati (and therefore handles), an absolute blast to ride and pretty good value makes it an almost impossible dream. Character, fun and style it has in bundles. I can't even think of a bike that comes close.'

Bike magazine, 1993, on the £7,200 Ducati Monster 900

Above: To keep costs down the Monster, famously, was a 'parts-bin special', using Ducati's 900SS engine, 888 frame and 750SS forks and brakes; only the tank and bodywork were new. (Ducati)

Right: Even its instruments were as minimal (and thus cheap) as possible. The result, however, was a stylish, fun and, crucially, affordable way into Ducati ownership. (Ducati)

The success of the original 900 led to a whole family of Monster spin-offs including a 600, 750 and, later, high-performance versions using the 888 engine and uprated cycle parts. (Ducati)

WHO LOVED IT?

Fun, fashionable, accessible and affordable, the Monster 900 was such a hit that it not only stabilised Ducati but spawned a whole Monster family that lives on to this day.

It only just made it into dealers, too. Galluzzi's boss, Massimo Bordi, was only begrudgingly encouraging, company hierarchy questioned the appeal of an unfaired Ducati and it was only when the prototype received a rapturous reception at the Milan Show that the decision was made to put it into production. Ducati was glad they did. An instant hit, the 900 Monster was such a success it was quickly followed with a raft of variants and spin-offs – first a 600, then a 750, then liquid-cooled, four-valve performance versions and more. In the noughties it received a total makeover and it lives on today as one of Ducati's most important machines. By 2021 it was estimated that in excess of 350,000 Monsters of all types had been sold.

And the name? According to Galluzzi himself, it actually came from his kids, after a small plastic toy that was popular at the time ... It suited the raw, red, aggressive Ducati just as well ...

YAMAHA YZF750R, 1993

Yamaha's 1993 YZF750R may have been late to the 750 superbike party, but it was probably the best of the bunch – great-looking with a free-revving 125bhp five-valve four and sweet handling, too. (Yamaha)

By 1993 Yamaha's sports bikes were on the slide. Not only had Honda's new FireBlade rendered its FZR1000 EXUP obsolete, Yamaha looked to have missed the 750 Superbike party, too. While its homologation special FZR750R OW-01 had some success, most heroically with Carl Fogarty's TT lap record in 1992, it hadn't matched Honda's RC30. And on the street, while Kawasaki had its ZXR750 and Suzuki its ageing GSX-R750, Yamaha had precisely ... nothing.

WHAT THEY SAID

'On paper or on asphalt the YZF750 adds up. As to its future on the race tracks of the world, it isn't a question of will it win, but how many times. If the YZF is as good on track as it is on the street Yamaha will need to clear a large spot on the trophy shelf.'

Sport Rider magazine, April 1994, on the $9,799 Yamaha YZF750R

A strip-shot reveals the gorgeous aluminium twin-spar frame, compact 749cc EXUP-equipped engine, massive six-piston brake calipers and state-of-the-art suspension. (Yamaha)

Sports cockpits don't get more definitively nineties. Classic three-dial asymmetrical analogue display, offset ignition switch, polished top yoke and straightforward switchgear. Note the 13,000rpm redline. (Yamaha)

The 1993 YZF750R changed all that – almost. New from the ground up, it was classic Yamaha FZR/YZF sportster: its 749cc five-valve, EXUP-equipped transverse four was a free-revving screamer with the most power in the class (125bhp); the gorgeous aluminium Deltabox frame gave ultra-nimble (for a four) handling; cycle parts included massive 320mm discs with *six* piston calipers plus fully adjustable inverted forks and shock and, with Yamaha's new 'foxeye' headlights and beautifully balanced styling, it was the best-looking 750, too.

Unfortunately, despite the addition of an even more alluring SP homologation special for racing, with solo seat, hot cams, flat-slide carbs, close-ratio gearbox, uprated suspension and alloy tank, it was all too late. Yes, Jamie Whitham creamed the 1993 British championship on his Fast Orange SP and Eddie Lawson the Daytona 200, but the YZF was never a success where it mattered most – WSB – and on the street its mantle had already been stolen by the 'Blade. Yamaha would have to wait for the 1998 R1 to reclaim that, but the YZF750R, today, is finally fondly remembered as one of the greatest 750 fours of all.

And if the standard YZF750R wasn't special enough for you, there was also the homologation special, race-spec SP version (rear) with solo seat, flat-slide carbs, uprated suspension and more. (Yamaha)

WHO LOVED IT?

Although a great bike, the late-arriving YZF was overshadowed by the FireBlade, wasn't a sales success and had already been dropped by the time Niall Mackenzie claimed his second (of three) British Superbike crowns aboard the SP version.

DUCATI 916, 1994

B uffs say a true motoring classic must be innovative, beautiful, exotic, expensive, exclusive and achieve genuine racing success. The 1994 Ducati 916 had all that and more. Much more.

Its single-sided swingarm and under-seat exhausts started a new design trend (even though its acclaimed designer Massimo Tamburini later admitted both were inspired by Honda's NR750); its striking, chisel-nosed purity won design plaudits across the globe; as Ducati's flagship it was exotic, expensive and exclusive and, by the end of the 1990s, it hadn't just won WSB - it dominated it, winning first time out in 1994 with British hero Carl Fogarty before reclaiming it four more times up to 2000, with three to Foggy alone.

The 916 was the creation of Italian design genius Massimo Tamburini (previously the 'Ta' at Bimota), although even he later admitted its single-sided swingarm and under-seat exhausts had been inspired by Honda's NR750. (Ducati)

Was any motorcycle of the 1990s more significant? More successful? More lusted after? Ducati's 1994 916 had it all - innovation, beauty, race success and exclusivity. (Ducati)

WHAT THEY SAID

'The 916 is an open invitation to enjoy state-of-the-art motorcycle thinking, engineering, design and performance. In the US it will carry list prices of $14,500, a thousand bucks more than last year's 888. You don't have to be a genius to figure out that anyone who cares about exotic motorcycles will find this a screaming deal.'

Cycle World magazine, July 1994, on the $14,500 Ducati 916

And yet, even though the 916 was the successor to Ducati's 888/851, which itself claimed a WSB hat-trick up to 1993, no one really predicted the scale of the 916's success.

Born out of Cagiva Design Director Massimo Tamburini's Cagiva Research Centre in San Marino, its development had been kept under wraps. The engine was the 'Desmoquattro' from the 888 but taken up to 916cc by a 2mm longer stroke, resulting in power going from 100 to 114bhp. While the whole chassis, despite the heavier, single-sided swingarm, was lighter (by 4kg), shorter (by 20mm) and sharper.

On the road some of that was a pain. The 916 was so sporty and uncompromising it was also cramped and uncomfortable. But on track, where the 916 was launched (at Misano in February 1994) and where it would rack up its greatest honours, it was pretty much unbeatable: its grunty, explosive and droningly evocative engine blending with ultra-nimble handling.

The press were blown away, *Bike* magazine boldly claiming 'Carl Fogarty WILL win the World Superbike Championship this year', even though the 916 itself wasn't deemed sufficiently significant to even be pictured on its cover (told you no one saw the 916 coming). On track,

The 916 pilot's riding position: slim, focused, extreme and ... simple. As a road bike, although effective, it was cramped and uncomfortable. But as a racer, nothing else came close. (Ducati)

The 916's world press launch took place at Misano, Italy, in February 1994 and it's fair to say they were blown away. *Bike* magazine were prompted to predict Carl Fogary would win the WSB title. They were right. (Ducati)

its rivals were even more vanquished: as well as Foggy's 1994 WSB title it won the 1994 American AMA superbike crown, 1995 British superbike series and more. In magazine polls the 916 swept the board, too.

The fact most motorcycling mortals couldn't afford one didn't really matter. The 916 was a strikingly beautiful 'poster bike' for a generation and today is revered as not just one of the best bikes of the 1990s but of all time.

WHO LOVED IT?

Although a huge success, the 916 wasn't built in the numbers many expect. Just 2,000 Monopostos were made in 1994 along with 700 Bipostos, 199 Ss and 310 SPs. In 1995 there were around 500 Monopostos, 2,000 Bipostos and 300 Sennas and over the course of the 916's life up to 1998 just thirty-eight Factory racers were made.

In fact, Foggy and the 916 did even better still. The British rider won back-to-back crowns in 1994–95 before leaving for Honda. Troy Corser made it a Ducati hat-trick in 1996 before a returning Foggy won again, here, in 1998 and again on the 996 version in 1999. (Ducati)

BMW R1100/1150GS, 1994

While BMW had already successfully reinvented its boxer in the early 1990s with the all-new R1100RS in 1993, the model that ultimately completely re-energised the German marque and put it on the path to dominance it enjoys to this day came a year later – the R1100GS.

Although a logical successor to BMW's previous, air-cooled, boxer-powered GS 'adventure tourers' - the monster trail bike category BM had invented with the 1980 R80G/S, before growing into the R100GS - the new 1100 did it in such a clever, cohesive and radical way it was like a GS from the future. The new oil-cooled, 80bhp, shaft drive boxer twin did without a conventional frame and instead had subframes front and rear; the 'Telelever' front suspension and 'Paralever' rear were quirky but effective; there were clever 'cross-spoke' wire wheels that allowed tubeless tyres; the big tank and 'duck bill' front bodywork gave it an utterly distinctive look; and even the switchgear bucked convention.

Despite the fact the GS was a 'slow burner', it grew to become a massive success story. The first update, the R1150GS, followed in 1999 and was even more successful. (BMW)

Although based on the same engine and frame (what there was of it) as the RS, the GS had different suspension, wheels, bodywork and riding position – but it quickly proved itself to be the more versatile machine. (BMW)

In truth, at first it was all so much that the GS was something of a 'slow burner'. But word of its immense practicality, versatility and class grew. An update into the even better (and even odder-looking) R1150GS in 1999 cemented its stature and the launch of the 2002 Adventure version, publicised famously by Ewan MacGregor and Charley Boorman's *Long Way Round* TV adventure, created a bestseller BMW has dined out on ever since – but it all started with the 1993 R1100GS.

WHAT THEY SAID

'It's got a comfortable, upright seating position, a comfy perch for a companion, stunning suspension, optional hard luggage and an engine you can see. Plus, you can corner the GS so hard you'll swear its oil-cooled cylinder heads will throw sparks. But they won't. This is one exceptional motorcycle.'

Cycle World, September 1994, on the $11,890 BMW R1100GS

WHO LOVED IT?

The R1100GS eventually became one of BMW's biggest sellers with 39,842 built between 1994 and 1999 and paved the way for even more success. The succeeding 1999 R1150GS did even better, selling 75,851 up to 2005.

At home whether on the dirt, on motorways or around town, the GS, especially in later 1200 then 1250 forms, became renowned as the most versatile of bikes and BMW's bestseller. (BMW)

BIMOTA SB6, 1994

With the arrival of fine-handling Japanese superbikes like Yamaha's EXUP and Honda's FireBlade, Italian reframing specialists seemed to have nowhere left to go, but there was time for one final hurrah – the SB6. (Bimota)

By the mid-1990s, the glory days of Italian chassis specialists Bimota were over. Everyone knew that. While 1980s Bimotas such as the exquisite 1982 KB2 Laser rehoused the most powerful Japanese supersport engine of the day – Kawasaki's GPz550 four – in a bespoke, monoshock street racer chassis complete with full race fairing and the best cycle parts money could buy, by the 1990s, the Japanese were producing fine-handling chassis of their own. Why buy a Bimota when you could have a FireBlade, EXUP or ZXR for half the price?

But Bimota did have one final hurrah – the 1994 SB6.

Based on Suzuki's 147bhp GSX-R1100, Bimota had chosen wisely. The big Gixxer was not only the most powerful superbike around, it was also pretty much the last of the old-style Japanese litre-plus sports bikes – big, heavy and with handling that could be more than a handful.

WHAT THEY SAID

'Interest in the SB6 is so intense that the factory is swamped with orders. After riding it that apparent commercial success is well and truly deserved. Prospective owners signed up for SB6s without ever riding one and I doubt very much that any will be disappointed once they have.'

Cycle World, March 1994, on the $20,000 Bimota SB6

The later SB6R (for Race) version, with revised styling and some technical updates, helped the Suzuki GSX-R1100-powered SB6 become the best-selling Bimota of all time. (Bimota)

The SB6 changed all that by doing what Bimota had always done best: the big engine was rehoused in Bimota's own rigid, compact and beautiful aluminium twin-spar frame, suspension and brakes were by Paioli and Brembo, and it was all clothed in exquisite, race-style bodywork with a twin-beam face.

The result was the best Bimota so far. Monstrously powerful yet purposefully compact, incredibly sharp steering for a 1100, beautiful, exotic and extremely desirable. The public thought so, too, making SB6 the best-selling Bimota so far and helping finance further forays such as the GSX-R750-engined SB7, TL1000-engined SB8 and ill-fated two-stroke V-Due. But if Bimota wasn't quite done yet, it'd never again hit the popularity heights of the SB6.

WHO LOVED IT?

The SB6 was built in two forms – the standard SB6, of which 1,144 were produced between 1994 and 1996, and the SB6R, from 1997 with new cams, bodywork changes and new clocks, of which 600 were made up to 1998. Together, the SB6 sold more than double any other Bimota.

After dominating the 125cc sportster class for so long, Italian lightweight specialists Aprilia arguably left it too late to produce its first 250 – but the RS250 was still spectacularly good. (Aprilia)

Talking of last hurrahs, there was surely no greater, or sadder, motorcycling swansong in the early to mid-1990s than that of the sports two-stroke, which was finally being regulated off the roads. And there was arguably no better or more fitting final example of the breed than Aprilia's 1994 RS250.

Following the likes of Kawasaki's KR-1S and Suzuki's RGV 250, Aprilia's first 250 GP replica took a typically Italian, more extreme approach. With its racing version challenging for the 250 GP crown with Max Biaggi, the RS was conceived as a road-going replica – right down to its optional 'Chesterfield' livery. The gorgeous polished aluminium twin-spar frame was its spitting image. Its cycle parts were Italian and the best in the class – Boge shock and Brembo brakes – and yet its engine choice was slightly odd – not by Rotax, as usual with Aprilias, but from the Suzuki RGV itself.

It didn't really matter. The RS250 looked gorgeous, with 72bhp and the best handling in the class, it went better and suddenly there was a new quarter-litre stroker king.

The exquisite aluminium frame was Aprilia's own, the brakes were by Brembo but the V-twin engine, despite what the clutch cover suggests, was from, of all makes, Suzuki – from the rival RGV250. (Aprilia)

WHAT THEY SAID

'You don't need to be Max Biaggi to ride the new RS250 but you do need to be to find much wrong with it. At the world launch of the stunning 250 at Misano the RS seemed to have it all: a fast motor; an exquisite chassis; and, perhaps more than anything, the looks and detailing worth flogging granny for.'

Bike magazine, April 1994, on the £5,495 Aprilia RS250

A restyle and update in 1997 brought the RS250 even closer to Aprilia's works GP racers, although its looks weren't liked by everyone and, by then, the 250 two-stroke class was running out of time. (Aprilia)

Except it was also all a bit too late. With prohibitive emissions regulations looming and production 250cc racing already on the decline, the RS250 was a great bike that arrived as the party was finishing. It lingered on into the early noughties and Aprilia even updated it in 1998, but by then it was already obsolete. But what a way for 250 strokers to bow out.

WHO LOVED IT?

Although exquisite, by 1994 the emissions regulations writing was on the wall for two-stroke sports bikes like the RS and Suzuki was already discounting its RGV250. Just 3,500 RS250s were made in its first year.

HONDA RVF750R (RC45), 1994

One of the most anticipated bikes of the 1990s was also one of its biggest disappointments. The RVF750R (RC45) was intended to succeed Honda's RC30 and reprise its production racing dominance. (Honda)

Cynics will say the RC45 wasn't the success it should have been in the 1990s. It never matched the racing roll of honour of its predecessor, the RC30; in stock trim its V4 motor produced just 118bhp when Yamaha's YZF already had seven more; and with a price tag of $27,500 in the US (£18,000 in the UK), it was prohibitively expensive. In fact, *Performance Bikes* magazine went so far as to brand it, in its cover test of June 1994, a 'waste of money'.

But neither was that the whole story. True, in superbike racing, Honda's 750cc V4 struggled to match the larger-capacity (1,000cc), lighter V-twins, particularly Ducati's all-conquering 916 – but it did have its moments. The WSB crown came via John Kocinski in 1997 and there were a couple of AMA crowns, but the RC45 shone brightest at the TT and in world endurance.

That 118bhp was something of a red herring. In full race-prepped, kitted form (the RC45 was a homologation special racer, after all), its output was nearer 150 and, although heavy compared to rival twins, its spec, including titanium rods and fuel injection, blew most rivals away. Sure, it wasn't the 'seachange' bike the RC30 had been, but it was still the most exquisite, advanced V4 racer ever built and remains a highly prized collectors' machine to this day.

WHAT THEY SAID

'True, the performance numbers are disappointing, but the engine's linear power delivery and stirring exhaust note almost make up for them. And the chassis, while not intended for freeway travel, is rock solid at hair-raising lean angles.'

Cycle World magazine, March 1994, on the £18,000 Honda RVF750R (RC45)

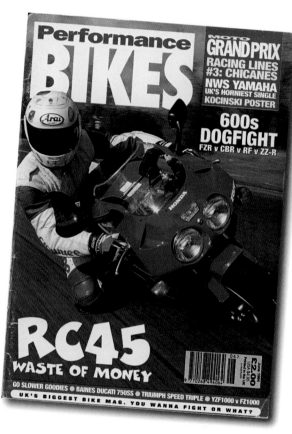

Unfortunately, although phenomenal, the RC45 didn't manage that race success and was also expensive. Leading UK magazine *Performance Bikes* put it more bluntly ... (Author's collection)

In the end, Honda's 'ultimate V4' managed just one WSB crown before Honda beat Ducati at its own game with the 2000 VTR1000 SP-1 V-twin. The V4 did fare better in endurance and roads racing, however. (Honda)

WHO LOVED IT?

Produced purely as an 'homologation special' for World Superbike racing, just 200 RC45s were built in 1994 (with only twenty going to the US and a further 500 made for the Japanese market). As a result, it's one of the rarest bikes ever built by Honda.

HONDA VFR750F, 1994

Honda's road-targeted V4 offering of 1994, the VFR750F, had none of the RC45's problems and quickly gained a reputation for being classy, with a fabulous engine and great all-round ability few came close to. (Honda)

It wasn't the fastest, most powerful, most tech-nologically advanced, lavishly equipped or even most expensive, but most motorcycle journalists will say the third-generation VFR750F, the M through final R versions from 1994 to 1998, was the best motorcycle of the 1990s.

A slick sports tourer powered by a peerless V4, it was an absolute triumph of refinement, quality and real-world usability. And its success was largely due to it being the third evolution of an already brilliant bike.

The first VFR750F-G came out in 1986 and was revolutionary: a no-expense spared Honda exercise in proving its V4 project after the failure of the original 1982/3 VF750S and F.

The new, 1994 VFR was effectively the third-generation version of the bike first launched in 1986 as the VFR750F-G and even that bike had been considered utterly classy and ahead of its time. (Honda)

A 'second-generation' VFR750F-L arrived in 1991, built on the original foundations with a new single-sided swingarm and extra refinement ... but also less power and more weight. (Honda)

WHAT THEY SAID

'I can't think of another bike that demands such miniscule nit-picking when looking to find fault. And that's because, basically, the VFR's got it all: an astonishing, distinctive engine; the best "compromise" chassis around and the highest quality of build, finish and integrated design of any bike on the road.'

Bike magazine, March 1994, of the £7,605 Honda VFR750F

That was fixed with the 1994 VFR750F-R – power was back up, weight was down, its Ferrari Testarossa-inspired styling was exquisite, and its build quality, class, refinement and versatility were without equal. (Honda)

The second, the VFR750F-L in 1990, was better yet, smoother, slicker and graced with the novel Pro-Arm single-sided swingarm. But the best, unquestionably, was the Mk III in 1994, which was not only classily beautiful with its NR750/Ferrari Testarossa-inspired styling, but 10kg lighter thanks to a new frame, swingarm, wheels and exhaust, yet still characterised by its rich, curdly, responsive 100bhp V4 delivery and distinctive exhaust note. It had utterly neutral and natural handling, sublime ergonomics and versatility, and an air of peerless class few motorcycles have approached since.

As one Honda PR man famously said at the time: 'I don't care how much it costs – it's worth three times as much.'

Other VFRs may have followed. But none were as complete and classy as the 1994 750F.

WHO LOVED IT?

Although not the fastest and pricier than most 750s, the VFR was also classy, capable and bulletproof, attracting a mature, discerning ownership. The last carb-fed VFR before the 1998 VFR800Fi, most consider it the ultimate incarnation of the breed.

KAWASAKI ZX-9R NINJA, 1994

Honda wasn't the only Japanese manufacturer making a 900 in the 1990s – Kawasaki's new ZX-9R Ninja sat between its ZXR750 and ZZ-R1100 and was a brilliant street-sport all-rounder. (Kawasaki)

In 1994, a decade after its revolutionary GPz900R and twenty years after its first 900cc Z1, Kawasaki came up with its own 900cc rival to the all-conquering Honda FireBlade, the ZX-9R Ninja – except, in reality, the new Kawasaki wasn't really a rival to the Honda at all.

Conceived as a power-packed, heavyweight sports *tourer*, the ZX-9R was instead positioned between Kawasaki's ZXR750 superbike and hyperbike ZZ-R1100 and blended elements from both (the ZX-9R's engine was a bored and stroked version of the ZXR's, the bolt-on rear subframe mimicked the ZZ-R's).

The result, with butch, macho styling, a screaming 139bhp, steadfast handling and full-sized proportions and comfort, was a great, fast, versatile road bike that became a Kawasaki bestseller, spawned a 600cc little brother, the ZX-6R, which was even more successful, and lived through numerous incarnations and updates right up to 2003.

WHAT THEY SAID

'The third Kawasaki 900 in 20 years isn't about to make the splash its forebears did. Not with GSX-Rs and FZRs in the world already. But like those models it's good enough to run and run.'

Superbike magazine, 1994, on the £8,095 Kawasaki ZX-9R Ninja

In fact, the new Ninja was so important for Kawasaki the Japanese firm even used its new World Superbike champion, Scott Russell, to help with its development and promotion. (Kawasaki)

Sporty yet substantial enough for two, 140+bhp fast, fine handling and good-looking, the ZX-9R Ninja lived on in Kawasaki's range, via a series of updates and facelifts, right up to 2004. (Kawasaki)

The ZX-9R may never have mustered any track success (Kawasaki had the ZXR750 for that) and may have been bigger and heavier than the revolutionary FireBlade, but that's missing the point. Instead, the 'Ninja 9' was a classy, ballistically fast sports all-rounder that was comfortable, capable of taking a pillion and, for legions of Kawasaki fans, more than enough. The ZX-9R might not have had the pizazz or made the same impact as Kawasaki 900 forebears such as the GPz and Z1, but it was a more than worthy addition to its 1990s line-up.

WHO LOVED IT?

Produced in five different versions between 1994 and 2003, the ZX-9R filled the gap between Kawasaki's ZXR750 and ZZ-R1100 and was admired for its lusty performance (peaking at 143bhp), real-world road manners and decent value.

TRIUMPH SPEED TRIPLE 900, 1994

1994's Speed Triple was revived Triumph's best bike so far, with bags of three-cylinder character, enough street performance and improved quality and finishes. Unfortunately, the same couldn't be said for Triumph's press pictures. (Triumph)

The 1991 relaunch of Triumph, after billionaire John Bloor's purchase of the liquidated brand followed by the creation of an all-new family of modern modular motorcycles in a brand-new factory in Hinckley, Leicestershire, was a genuine 1990s British biking success story. But, at first at least, as the firm concentrated on establishing its engineering and reliability, it was also an overly conservative one. While the three-cylinder versions of its new engine stood out against the blander four, the Trident roadster also had far more character than the Daytona sportster and Trophy tourer.

The 1994 Speed Triple 900, however, an unfaired café racer based on the Daytona but with the triple engine, was something new: a street sportster that didn't have to compete with the Japanese – a bike bristling with character, with a great name and hints of heritage (the name was inspired by the original 1936 Speed Twin) and with a glossy, bold yellow, orange or black livery made possible by Hinckley's new paint shop.

But it was undoubtedly at its best in all black. A one-make race series, the Speed Triple Challenge, plus an uncharacteristically bullish ad campaign helped, too. (Triumph)

In truth, the Speed Triple was also something of a 'parts bin special' with ingredients from other Triumph bikes, while its inspiration remains something of a mystery. Some say Italian Triumph importer (and serial specials builders) Numero Tre came up with the idea. Others that it was an in-house creation (which the name certainly was).

WHAT THEY SAID

'Nothing I've ridden so perfectly captures the minimalist appeal of the cafe-racer concept. And in spite of having been developed around Triumph's modular engineering approach, the Speed Triple is the most distinctive, hard-edged and individual of the four models making up Triumph's three-cylinder 750/900cc range.'

Cycle World magazine, February 1994, on the £7,600 Triumph Speed Triple

WHO LOVED IT?

Just 1,421 examples of the original 900 were built but the bike was so successful and inspirational it spawned the whole Speed Triple family, which remains a Triumph cornerstone with over 35,000 of all types having been built since.

What's beyond doubt is that the Speed Triple stood out like no Hinckley Triumph had before. It became an instant hit and (partly thanks to a popular one-make race series and advertising campaign involving a Rottweiller), put Triumph on the map and paved the way for the more distinctive, characterful bikes that followed. As Triumph today admits: it was the Speed Triple that gave new Triumph its mojo.

YAMAHA XJR1200, 1994

Speaking of 'bullish' ... Few 1990s motorcycles were as meaty, brutish and radiated as much machismo as Yamaha's XJR1200. The best of a new 'retro roadster' class, it was popular into the 2010s. (Yamaha)

One of the biggest biking trends of the mid-1990s was retro-roadsters – Japanese 1970s style, four-cylinder, upright 'twin shockers' with (mostly) modern engines, brakes, suspension and so on. And, of them all (and there was a lot), Yamaha's beefy, burly XJR1200 was the best.

At the XJR's heart was a modernised version of the grunty, air-cooled four from the old FJ1200 but everything else was (updated) 1970s 'old school' – twin dials, shocks, styling and more. (Yamaha)

As with many biking trends, it started in Japan. Kawasaki came up with its first Zephyr 400 for the home market in 1989 before launching 550 and 750 versions into Europe in 1991; Honda had its CB400 Super Four, and Yamaha its XJR400 from 1993, which it followed up with the 'export' 1200 from 1994.

Opposite: The XJR proved so successful it was updated to XJR1300 form in 1999, also gaining improved 'blue spot' brakes. An SP version, complete with uprated Ohlins suspension, was also available. (Yamaha)

'It's half Zephyr, half CB1000 and half a great big dollop of lunatic Yamaha spirit. And if that lot adds up to a bike and a half then that's because that's what the XJR1200 is.'

Bike magazine, August 1995, on the £7,625 XJR1200

But while the Kawasakis had charm, they lacked performance, attitude and were only a marginal success. The XJR1200, on the other hand, with its grunty, 98bhp FJ1200-derived engine, black paint, twin Ohlins rear shocks, 11.7sec quarter mile and 145mph performance, had it in spades.

Yes, it was heavy and a little crude, but the XJR was great-looking, comfortable, easy to ride, handled, took a pillion and was even reasonably practical. Best of all, it genuinely rekindled the spirit of the 1970s and was a hooliganistic hoon when you wanted it to be.

All of that made the XJR the most successful Japanese 'retro' of all, spawn an SP version in 1997, grow into 1300 form in 1999, inspire rivals such as Suzuki's GSX-1400 and Honda's CB1300 and ultimately live on right up to 2018.

WHO LOVED IT?

Who wanted an XJR? Anyone wanting classic, 1970s-style 'UJM's (Universal Japanese Motorcycle), twin-shock roadsters with a big four-cylinder motor – but modern engineering, suspension and brakes.

TRIUMPH THUNDERBIRD 900, 1995

One of the most significant new Triumphs of the 1990s was also one of the least heralded. The 1995 Thunderbird was the Hinckley firm's first true 'retro' (years before the Bonneville) and key to its success in the US. (Triumph)

While the Japanese did 'retros' first in the early 1990s – with their 1970s-style, four-cylinder roadsters – the revival of Triumph and the success of its heritage-flavoured Speed Triple and its impending relaunch into the USA prompted another retro style: the classically British-styled Thunderbird 900.

WHAT THEY SAID

'It represents the outlook of Triumph's corporate rearview mirror, a nod to heritage and to a perceived, and apparently real, American appetite for nostalgia. It's a stunningly good vintage bike, if that's really what you want. If you want a more modern motorcycle, well, Triumph builds those, too.'

Cycle World magazine, May 1995, on the $9,995 Triumph Thunderbird 900

Launched a full six years before its first Bonneville, the T-bird was a modern, three-cylinder roadster based on the Trident 900 but with completely new (old?) styling to appeal to an American market inspired by classic 1960s and '70s Triumphs.

Although effectively a restyled Trident 900, the T-bird was impressively executed, with restyled/retuned engine, quality cycle parts and impressive detailing. It remained on sale into the 2000s. (Triumph)

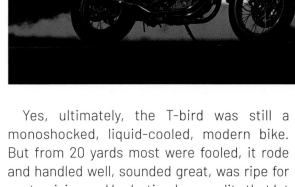

It was executed impressively well, too. There was a new, rounded tank with optional two-tone paint and classic 'mouth-organ' badge, quality alloy-rimmed Akront wire wheels and lots of chrome, but the masterstroke was the comprehensive restyling of the liquid-cooled triple, with fins, new curvy cases and more. It was even detuned to 85bhp to give a more grunty, cruiser-style ride.

WHO LOVED IT?

Although targeted at the US, Hinckley Triumph's first 'retro' was popular globally, spawned variants including the Adventurer, Thunderbird Sport and Legend, and remained in production from 1994 to 2003.

Yes, ultimately, the T-bird was still a monoshocked, liquid-cooled, modern bike. But from 20 yards most were fooled, it rode and handled well, sounded great, was ripe for customising and had a timeless quality that let it live on well into the noughties.

Today, most think the revived 2001 Triumph Bonneville put the British retro on the map. In truth, the 'Bonnie' might never have been recreated at all without the preceding Thunderbird.

KTM 620 DUKE, 1995

Austrian off-road specialist KTM made its first concerted inroads into the road-bike market with the 620 Duke – essentially an enduro bike but with road-bike, 'supermoto' wheels, brakes and bodywork. (KTM)

Today Austrian brand KTM enjoys a reputation as the nuttiest of motorcycle manufacturers. It calls its mad-cap 170bhp 1290 Super Duke 'The Beast'; its big 'Super Adventure' bikes are about as hard core as the breed gets; while its single-cylinder 125 and 390, and twin-cylinder 790 and 890 Duke roadsters are simply bonkers.

But they can all trace their success back to the 1990s and the creation of the first KTM Duke – the 1995 620.

In the early 1990s KTM was still, almost exclusively, an off-road motorcycling specialist, with an admired but necessarily niche range of motocross and enduro machines. The 620 Duke changed all that.

Inspired by the early 1990s popularity of home-brewed 'supermotos' (street bikes converted from motocrossers) and created initially as a 1993 concept bike derived from KTM's biggest-engined enduro of the time, the Duke had a sufficiently positive response to encourage KTM bosses to put it into limited production.

WHAT THEY SAID

'It's a motorcycle for people who understand the allure of a performance single, who like to be different, who want a bike with balls and, if you hurry, there might just be a few left that are unspoken for.'

Cycle World magazine, September 1995, on the $7,900 KTM 620 Duke

At the Duke's heart was KTM's then biggest engine – a 620cc, liquid-cooled single good for around 50bhp. The side-panel slogan of 'Single Piston Performance' says everything else you need to know ... (KTM)

Great-looking, fun, good at stunts and different, the Duke was sufficiently successful to start KTM on a whole new path. Dukes still form a significant part of its output today. (KTM)

The result was the 1995 620 Duke with a 55bhp, 609cc single in modified enduro frame. Beefy 40mm inverted forks, street-sized 17in wire wheels and big Brembo were added, the whole thing wrapped in new, mean-looking plastics and the public advised to stand well back.

Although expensive, impractical and unproven, they didn't – the Duke was such a hoot and hit that it set KTM on a whole new path it's still following (and behaving badly on) to this day ...

WHO LOVED IT?

The 620 Duke didn't sell enormously but KTM's first road bike with a four-stroke engine had such a nutty appeal and strong image that it effectively changed the Austrian firm's direction, leading to today's Duke-dominated road-bike range.

APRILIA MOTO 6.5, 1995

Not all radical attempts at new-style singles were successful, however. Aprilia's wacky Moto 6.5 was also a bold 650cc single – but was styled by a kitchenware designer and not much good for anything. (Aprilia)

Some memorable 1990s motorcycles were created by legendary designers, such as the Ducati 916 by Massimo Tamburini. Others by inspired but otherwise unknown engineers, such as the Honda FireBlade by Tadao Baba. But one was the fruit of a celebrated kitchenware stylist with no previous experience of bikes at all ...

In the early 1990s, upstart Italian manufacturer Aprilia was riding a wave of innovative success. Its racy 125s were the poster bikes of a teen generation; its racers seemed unstoppable and its stylish scooters were sweeping all before them. But company patriarch Ivano Beggio wanted more - specifically a stylish, urban statement that might become as famous as Piaggio's Vespa.

For an iconic look, he eschewed conventional engineers (the Vespa had been created by an aircraft designer, after all) and turned to French style celebrity Philippe Starck, most famous for his rocket-shaped juicer. With a starting point of Aprilia's 650 Pegaso trailie and a brief to create an urban runabout that would appeal to non-motorcyclists, the Moto 6.5 was the result.

It wasn't a success. Starck's stylised, 'no compromise' approach resulted in poor handling due to an oddly positioned exhaust; Starck himself alienated Aprilia's own design engineers, leaving only Beggio convinced by the project; there were production difficulties; it was badly received by the press; it had only 45bhp and was not much use for anything.

Even so, the Moto 6.5 remained in production for two years, is still immediately identifiable and, today, is regarded as something of an appreciating design icon. Sort of.

Aprilia's hope had been for a style-setting city runabout. What they were left with was a bike that went out of production after just a couple of years. Today they're becoming collectable, though. (Aprilia)

WHO LOVED IT?

'Loved' might be a bit strong – but the Moto 6.5 still generates strong feelings, is appreciated for its bold quirkiness and is becoming a modern classic – especially as only around 6,500 were ever made.

SUZUKI GSF600N BANDIT, 1995

Suzuki's huge-selling GSF600N Bandit proved radical concepts weren't necessary for success. But if you offered good all-round performance in a conventional package at a great price it could be a winner. (Suzuki)

ost great bikes of the 1990s were the result of genius design creating extravagant, exotic machinery, but a handful were more prosaic: machines for the masses created from mostly existing components whose genius was being the right bike, at the right price, at the right time. An example of the latter that stands out in the 1990s more than any other is the 1995 Suzuki 600 Bandit.

WHAT THEY SAID

'Suzuki has crafted a terrific all-around motorcycle all the while keeping its price at an acceptable level. It does nearly everything well and almost nothing poorly. The 600S is, in many ways, the very motorcycle *Cycle World* asked for six years ago. It was a very good idea then. It's a very good bike now.'

Cycle World magazine, July 1995, on the £3,999 Suzuki GSF600N Bandit

The Bandit's engine was from the obsolete GSX-600F supersports and its cycle parts were from the parts bin. But it looked good, was fun and versatile (for a roadster) and cost just £3,999! (Suzuki)

The naked 600 Bandit was also joined by other versions, including an even more practical, half-faired GSF600S, plus two bruising but brilliant 1200 versions, the GSF1200N and S. (Suzuki)

On paper, it didn't seem anything to get excited about. Bandits, bare-bones four-cylinder Suzuki roadsters, were nothing new with a Japanese market 400cc version imported briefly, underwhelmingly, in 1991. The new 600's ingredients of old 78bhp oil-cooled motor from the now uncompetitive GSX-600F supersports, tubular steel frame and off-the-peg cycle parts promised little more.

Overall, the 600 Bandit was so successful it inspired rivals from Yamaha (FZS600 Fazer), Honda (CB600F Hornet) and Kawasaki (ZR-7), together creating a new budget middleweight class. (Suzuki)

And yet ... it all gelled beautifully. As a real-world, upright roadster, the 600 Bandit's performance was both sufficient and hooliganistic fun, it was comfortable, practical, stylish and had enough neat touches (such as twin chrome-rimmed clocks) to satisfy, and, crucially, at just £3,999, when the latest supersports were over five, it was a steal.

WHO LOVED IT?

The Bandit was versatile, fun and, above all, cheap, making it such a huge sales hit that rivals Yamaha and Honda were forced to respond with their Fazer and Hornet 600s. Updated repeatedly, it remained on sale for over twenty years.

After *Bike* magazine put it on its cover with the tag 'Laughing all the way to the bank', the Bandit became such a bestseller it spawned a whole new budget class that went on to include Yamaha's Fazer and Honda's Hornet. An equally successful bigger brother, the 1200 Bandit, along with half-faired versions followed quickly and Suzuki's Bandit family went to live through three generations up to 2016. But the original 1995 600 was the best. No bike has been better named.

3

PERFORMANCE GOES UP A PEG

In the second half of the 1990s the major manufacturers seemed to embrace a new boldness. Suzuki, for one, replaced its loved but ageing GSX-R750 with an all-new, grand prix-inspired version. (Suzuki)

HONDA CBR1100XX SUPER BLACKBIRD, 1996

The all-new CBR1100XX was Honda's no holds barred attempt to wrest the 'world's fastest' crown – even its nickname, 'Super Blackbird', was inspired by the world air speed record-holding Lockheed SR-71 Blackbird. (Honda)

By 1996 Kawasaki's 'king of speed', the ZZ-R1100, had reigned as the world's fastest production motorcycle for over half the decade. But it was about to be comprehensively blown away by one of the greatest bikes of the 1990s – Honda's CBR1100XX Super Blackbird.

Conceived specifically to seize the 'world's fastest' crown, Honda's new hyperbike was a clean-sheet, no expense- or effort-spared design. Although the four-cylinder engine was developed from that of the FireBlade, much of it was all new and, displacing 1,137cc, was the largest CBR so far, producing a whopping 164bhp – 17 more than the Kawasaki. The huge, twin-spar aluminium frame was new too: rigid, long and utterly stable, and all clothed in ultra-slippery new aerodynamic bodywork developed in a wind tunnel.

WHAT THEY SAID

'Honda blows onto the scene with the fastest motorcycle ever produced. The CBR1100XX has set an even higher standard in the open-class sport-bike market, blending comfort and handling into a fast and refined package.'

Sport Rider magazine, February 1997, on the $11,499 Honda CBR1100XX Super Blackbird

It worked, of course – and then some – lofting the new record speed to 177mph and re-emphasising the point by launching the bike to the world's press at Paul Ricard circuit in southern France, famous for its Mistral Straight, the longest in bike sport.

At the heart of Honda's new super-slippery monster was an enlarged 1,137cc transverse four-cylinder engine derived from that of the CBR900RR FireBlade and producing a whopping 164bhp. (Honda)

The massive, beefy twin spare frame, however, was all new and designed to keep the CBR as stable as possible. (Note the massive ram air intakes at the bike's front end.) (Honda)

The narrow nose and slippery bodywork was developed in the wind tunnel with the primary aim of achieving a world-beating top speed. It worked, too, leap-frogging Kawasaki's ZZ-R1100 to 178mph. (Honda)

But although its reign didn't last long, swiped by Suzuki's GSX-1300R Hayabusa in 1999, the Blackbird was also much more than just the king of speed. Classy, comfortable, versatile and durable, it was also a superlative hyper-sports tourer and improved further in 1999 with fuel injection, larger tank and built-in immobiliser. That bike was so good it lived on to 2005 and remains relevant and revered to this day.

WHO LOVED IT?

A superfast, classy, 'gentleman's express', the Blackbird was on sale until 2005 and, with a first intended successor canned and the 2010 VFR1200F a failure, good used examples remain in demand up to this day.

SUZUKI GSX-R750WT SRAD, 1996

Suzuki's 1996 GSX-R750WT represented a clean sheet for the iconic but ageing GSX-R. Out went the signature cradle frame, in came a GP-inspired twin-beam, ram air and aerodynamic profile. (Suzuki)

The SRAD was not only the famous Suzuki GSX-R's return to form after losing its way in the early to mid-1990s, it was also the last great 750cc superbike of the decade.

A bold, clean-sheet design that finally replaced the Gixxer's traditional cradle frame for the then-dominant twin-spar design, the SRAD was Suzuki's bid to return to the top of the superbike tree. And, with inspiration from Kevin Schwantz's RGV500 GP, with which it shared many dimensions, a screaming, ram air-assisted transverse four (SRAD stood for Suzuki Ram Air Direct) that produced 128bhp at a heady 12,000rpm (the highest in the class), ultra-nimble steering and an aerodynamic profile that included a distinctive seat hump, it very nearly succeeded.

The result shared many of the dimensions of Suzuki's RGV500 GP bike as ridden to the world championship in 1993 by Kevin Schwantz in being ultra-compact and nimble. (Suzuki)

The distinctively bulbous removable pillion seat hump, meanwhile, was wind tunnel developed to maximise the new GSX-R's aerodynamic wind-cheating ability. (Suzuki)

Nearly, that is, but not quite. On the street, the SRAD quickly established itself as the sportiest 750, but in a class already dominated by Honda's FireBlade and shortly to be revolutionised further by Yamaha's upcoming R1, it struggled to stand out.

While on track, despite Suzuki's best efforts (and a number of race wins) it failed to usurp Ducati's all-dominant 916 in WSB.

WHAT THEY SAID

'Nimble handling, light weight, strong brakes and a powerful and flexible engine has turned Suzuki's GSX-R750 into the premier benchmark superbike.'

Superbike magazine, December 1997, on the £8,999 Suzuki GSX-R750T SRAD

On the whole, it all worked: the SRAD was the most powerful (128bhp), fastest, most nimble 750 four superbike yet – but it was still not enough to beat Ducati's 916 in WSB. (Suzuki)

The SRAD wasn't a complete failure, of course. It fared better in BSB and world endurance, spawned a popular 600cc supersports little brother and paved the way for the 2000 GSX-R1000, which would kick-start a whole new GSX-R dynasty, but rather than be the 750 king Suzuki hoped for, it was more the last hurrah for the 750 superbike.

WHO LOVED IT?

Not enough, to be honest. Although overnight the fastest 750 superbike, the SRAD still couldn't dethrone Ducati's 916 in WSB, while on the street it was quickly overshadowed by Yamaha's 1998 R1. Today, however, its 'first modern GSX-R' symbolism gives it modern classic status.

TRIUMPH T595 DAYTONA, 1997

After the 'first-generation' modular triples and fours with which Triumph relaunched as a brand in 1992, the Daytona T595 was the British marque's first clean-sheet design. (Triumph)

Although the 1990s return of Triumph had been a revelation and great success, its early bikes, based on a modular system of interchangeable, heavyweight triples and fours in fairly crude but solid chassis, were never truly competitive with the best from Europe and Japan.

That changed with the 1997 T595 Daytona. Hinckley Triumph's first clean-sheet, bespoke design, the T595 (the internal model name was found to confuse the public so was quickly dropped) was conceived as a road sportster rather than potential racer but, even so, was a quantum leap over all Triumphs before. The engine was an all-new triple developed with Lotus and featuring French Sagem fuel injection. The frame was a gorgeous polished aluminium tubular affair with a Ducati 916-style single-sided swingarm, while its curvaceous, sultry bodywork was styled by Britain's own John Mockett.

The result looked gorgeous and sounded even better, handled well, if slightly heavy, and, with 128bhp, good for over 160mph and largely competitive with the best, anywhere.

Although good enough to be a great success, in all honesty the T595 wasn't perfect. There were fuel injection and frame problems that prompted a recall; that 128bhp and hefty weight meant it was never quite in the same bracket as sportier rivals; and it was also out-sold, surprisingly so at first, by its 'naked' roadster brother, the T509 Speed Triple, which went on to outlive the Daytona and become the bedrock of Triumph's future range.

But that bike wouldn't have existed without the T595. The Daytona itself was improved and updated up to 2004, and today it's remembered as the bike with which new Triumph 'came of age'.

It impressed, too: an all-new tubular alloy frame held a single-sided swingarm, a new 128bhp, fuel-injected three-cylinder engine, decent cycle parts and swoopy all-new bodywork. (Triumph)

WHAT THEY SAID

'Last year's road tests of the new-generation three-cylinder sportbike all read pretty much the same: "Gorgeous motorcycle ... giant leap forward for the revitalized British firm ... shame about the flawed fuel injection, spongy suspension and the exhaust header that grounds in right-hand turns." To their credit, Triumph's R&D staff took each of these criticisms to heart. The result is a host of changes that makes it a noticeably improved motorcycle.'

Cycle World magazine, January 1998, on the £9,995 Triumph T595 Daytona

Even the Daytona's dash was state of the art: a sporty, white-faced, three-dial set-up bordered by a carbon-fibre panel holding the usual array of warning lights. (Triumph)

The result, although never intended as a track machine and despite being overshadowed by Yamaha's new R1, was enough for 'new Triumph' to start being taken very seriously. (Triumph)

WHO LOVED IT?

Although a success, T595 sales were hit by Yamaha's R1 and the expensive frame recall, and also by its T509 Speed Triple sister bike, which significantly outsold the Daytona. Even so, modern Triumph wouldn't be the same without it.

Bimota's radical V-Due promised much – a 500GP-style two-stroke for the street with Bimota's first in-house engine, fuel injection and an ultra-nimble chassis. Unfortunately, it didn't work out that way ... (Bimota)

Depending on who you ask, the Bimota V-Due was either one of the ultimate bikes of the 1990s or a disaster that caused the Italian brand's collapse.

In truth, it was probably both.

Conceived as the ultimate sports two-stroke, a 500cc GP-alike V-twin for the road with a claimed 110bhp but weighing just 136kg dry, its masterstroke was in being a two-stroke but with fuel injection and electronic ignition to combat the emissions regulations that were killing off the breed.

The fly in the ointment, however, especially for a small firm, was that, to create it, Bimota for the first time had to build its own engine and that, along with production delays and cash-flow problems, meant the bike wasn't fully developed. Injection problems resulted in expensive recalls; the planned 500-bike production run was never fulfilled with only around 340 built, and instead of being the saviour of the two-stroke engine, the V-Due became the bike that killed off Bimota in 1999.

Although the V-Due's chassis, style and performance potential were mouth-watering, engine and production problems hampered performance, reliability and deliveries. (Bimota)

WHAT THEY SAID

'Nothing but nothing on two wheels with a licence plate gives such a thrill as straddling the 500V-Due and gassing it hard. After being all but legislated out of existence the two-stroke is back – and the Bimota 500 V-Due is the proof.'

Superbike magazine, July 1997, on the £14,000 Binota V-Due

Ultimately, only a few hundred were built, the bulk having to revert to conventional carbs, and the financial strain drove Bimota into bankruptcy. Surviving V-Dues, however, are hugely collectable. (Bimota)

The V-Due wasn't a complete disaster, of course. When it ran it was exquisite; later bikes were sorted, mostly with the substitution of carbs. Bimota itself was revived in 2003 and the V-Due, today, is one of the most prized and collectable of all its bikes.

But, when launched in 1997, the V-Due was both a diamond and a disaster – hasn't that always been the way with Bimota?

WHO LOVED IT?

Just 185 examples of the original fuel-injected V-Due were built, along with twenty-six special 'Trofeo' models for a one-make series, 141 'Evoluzione' models, fourteen 'Corsa Evoluzione' bikes and twenty-two of the last version, the 'Edizione Finale'. All except the original 185 were fitted with carburettors.

HONDA VTR1000 FIRESTORM, 1997

The resurgence of Ducati's V-twins through the 1990s led to a series of Japanese 'imitations' – Yamaha had its TRX850, Suzuki the TL1000, while Honda's offering was the VTR1000F Firestorm, called the Super Hawk in the US. (Honda)

For a brief few years in the mid to late 1990s many of the Japanese manufacturers became obsessed with emulating Ducati. It was understandable. The Italian marque's 916 was dominating WSB, its air-cooled street V-twin sportsters had become fashionable and its Monster roadster was an urban style icon.

In response, Yamaha came up with its 900SS-alike 1995 TRX850 (albeit with a parallel not Vee twin engine), Honda its 'mini monster' 1997 VTR250, both of which were initially only available in Japan (although a Euro version of the TRX was made from 1996), while Suzuki was about to unleash its controversial TL1000S.

The most successful, however, was Honda's VTR1000 Firestorm. Launched in 1997, it was an all-new, liquid-cooled, V-twin road sportster and, with no racing aspirations (that would come later with the 2000 VTR1000 SP-1), typical Honda refinement, practicality and sweet ergonomics, it was all the better for it.

Its 996cc, 97bhp V-twin was a flexible, immaculately fuelled peach, its twin-spar frame and decent cycle parts gave light, sweet handling, it was good-looking, comfortable and versatile – and an instant hit.

WHAT THEY SAID

'It's the Japanese company's answer to the entire emerging class of high-performance V-twins, a preemptive strike against everything from Harley's yet-to-be-seen-in-production VR1000 to the hugely acclaimed Ducati 916 to the soon-to-be-released Aprilia RS 1000V.'

Cycle World magazine, December 1996, on the £7,995 Honda VTR1000

Sporty yet slim (although a later update provided a larger fuel tank), the VTR was also manageable, characterful, refined and well put together. (Honda)

Never intended for the track, the 100bhp V-twin proved a great road sportster popular into the 2000s. For racing success Honda would turn to the 2000 VTR1000 SP-1. (Honda)

Updates including a larger tank, more upright riding position plus dash and indicator tweaks followed in 2001. It lived on until 2005 and today it remains a solid, all-round road sportster, with a flavour of Italy ...

WHO LOVED IT?

The most versatile and reassuring of the Japanese V-twins, the Firestorm (Super Hawk in the US) was also the most successful, remaining in production until 2005, with an estimated 20,000 built.

APRILIA RSV1000 MILLE, 1998

Another firm keen to replicate the track and street success of Ducati's 916 was ambitious Italian brand Aprilia. The result was the RSV1000 Mille powered by a Rotax-developed 60-degree V-twin. (Aprilia)

The Japanese weren't the only ones in the mid to late 1990s trying to 'do a Ducati' – an upstart Italian brand wanted a slice of the Bologna firm's action, too.

By 1995 previously lightweight specialists Aprilia were probably the most dynamic, ambitious Italian motorcycle manufacturer of all. Its racy 125s were dominating the quarter-litre class, its recent RS250 was the best of its type and in racing it was sweeping all before it. Now was the time to 'go big'.

WHAT THEY SAID

'Aprilia's RSV Mille has the performance potential to put V-twin sportbikes back atop the heap and do it emphatically. Here is one of those rare serious sportbikes that can do it all – commuter duty, canyon shredder, and sport-tourer – without whupping the rider into submission, or forcing him to adapt to various idiosyncrasies.'

Cycle World magazine, December 1998, on the $13,799 Aprilia RSV Mille

Although bigger, taller and heavier than the 916, the RSV was still a fine, if slightly top-heavy, handler, but compensated to a degree by having more power – 128bhp. (Aprilia)

The resulting RSV1000 Mille was an all-new 1000cc V-twin superbike with its sights firmly set on Ducati's 916. On paper it had it all. Its 60-degree V-twin was created by Rotax and produced a 916-beating 128bhp, its alloy twin-spar frame was a work of art and held quality, and the multi-adjustable suspension and brakes and build quality were excellent, too. On the road it had the 916 beat, being more flexible, roomier, quicker and with real-world handling.

Unfortunately, it never did quite beat the 916 where it mattered most – on track. The Aprilia's higher CofG and roomier proportions made it more of a handful and, despite the homologation special SP version's adjustable frame, Ohlins, Brembos and shorter-stroke engine, it never did claim the WSB crown Aprilia craved so much.

It made a great, underrated road bike, though – and was a brilliant value used buy for years to come.

Even so, an unproven record, unconvincing styling and a high price meant that the Mille (and subsequent spin-off models including the Futura and Caponord) was not the sales success hoped for. (Aprilia)

WHO LOVED IT?

Although impressive and effective, the Mille (and later spin-off models such as the sports-tourer Futura and adventure Caponord) were never the commercial success hoped for, contributing to Aprilia's collapse in 2005. The higher-spec R and SP, however, are highly collectable today.

Even a top-spec, short-stroke, homologation special racing version, complete with Ohlins suspension, couldn't depose the 916 – but has since become something of a modern classic. (Aprilia)

YAMAHA FZS600 FAZER, 1998

The huge sales success of the bargain GSF600 Bandit meant it was inevitable that Suzuki's Japanese rivals would come up with their own versions. Yamaha's was the FZS600 Fazer. (Yamaha)

Suzuki's inspired and great value 1995 600 Bandit was such a success it was never likely to be the sole bike of its type – and, sure enough, rivals from Honda (1998 CB600F Hornet), Yamaha (1998 FZS600 Fazer) and Kawasaki (1999 ZR-7) all appeared before long using the same formula of an ageing, existing engine in a budget, largely 'parts bin' chassis.

But the Fazer was undoubtedly the best.

Based around a restyled, detuned YZF600R Thundercat engine producing 95bhp, in a new, tubular steel frame, with decent brakes and

WHAT THEY SAID

'When you push the Fazer to the limit, which is easy with those "Blue Dot" R1 brakes upfront, it dives a little bit and loads up the front end. It waggles a bit, but the handling is generally confidence-inspiring and if you take it steady you could ride to Budapest and feel no severe aches or pains.'

Motorcycle News, April 1998, on the £4,950 Yamaha FZS600 Fazer

suspension, a practical, upright riding position and useful half-fairing, the Fazer was Yamaha's take on the Bandit recipe – but beat it on all counts. It was more powerful, had better handling and braking, was more versatile thanks to its fairing – and was better looking, too.

The Fazer was based around a repurposed, restyled YZF600R Thundercat engine but with its own bespoke, Bandit-alike, budget tubular steel frame with 'parts bin' cycle parts. (Yamaha)

It was enough for the Yamaha to become an instant bestseller, as well, primarily to those looking for an affordable, unintimidating first big bike after passing their test, and at the same time made the Suzuki instantly seem obsolete (prompting an update of its own in 2000).

While Honda's offering, the madcap, CBR600F-engined Hornet, was also a strong seller and the Kawasaki was a worthy, cut-price commuter, if you wanted an affordable middleweight all-rounder in the late 1990s, there really could be only one ...

The Fazer was, however, offered in just one, faired version, complete with distinctive twin headlights. Its brakes were also a standout feature – being off-the-peg, top-quality 'blue spot' items. (Yamaha)

The result was sportier and better looking than the Bandit: more powerful, sharper steering and better braked – yet all, still, at a bargain price. No wonder it, too, was a bestseller. (Yamaha)

WHO LOVED IT?

Like Suzuki's 600 Bandit before it, the Fazer was fun, versatile and, above all, affordable – and better in virtually every respect, too. The recipe made it a big success, receiving a facelift in 2002, then being replaced by the all-new FZ6 Fazer in 2004, which remained in production until 2009.

Suzuki's late-1990s take on the V-twin road sportster promised to be the best of the bunch. Its all-new V-twin engine was punchy and powerful, its chassis appeared capable and it looked good, too. (Suzuki)

Of all the Japanese Ducati V-twin clones of the late 1990s, Suzuki's TL1000S should have been the best. Instead, although having a powerhouse of a motor so good it was pinched by Bimota for its SB8 WSB winner, then went on to be the bedrock of many of Suzuki's bikes well into the twenty-first century, it was blighted by rear suspension so bad the TL became referred to as 'the widowmaker'.

In truth, it wasn't really that bad and was also very nearly supreme. At its launch, its novel rotary rear damper was noticed to overheat causing waywardness. This, combined with the punchy motor and stumpy, tank-slapper prone steering, gave rise to scare stories that simply got out of hand, prompted a recall for a steering damper and ultimately destined the TL1000S to failure and deletion after just four years on sale.

WHAT THEY SAID

'The TL1000S was introduced only to face unexpected competition in the form of the Honda VTR1000; next the mysterious "death wobble" scandal led to another expensive recall but none of it was enough to keep Suzuki from bouncing back with the TL1000R.'

Motor Cyclist magazine, September 1998, on the $9,499 TL1000R

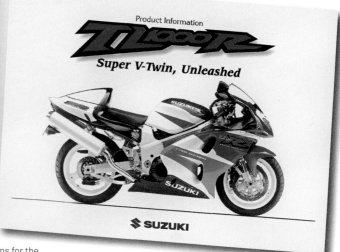

After the disaster of the TL1000S there were high expectations for the even sportier, beam-framed, fully faired TL1000R. Unfortunately, that bike, too, failed to live up to expectations. (Suzuki)

With flawed rear suspension, punchy performance and sharp steering, the S generated 'tank slapper' scare stories, prompting a recall. Today, however, it's considered a connoisseurs' classic. (Suzuki)

A second version, the more track sports, beam-framed TL1000R in 1998, fared better, but was also odd looking and too big and heavy for the WSB success Suzuki craved. Today, however, their lively engines, striking style and 'charismatic' rides are respected and their status has evolved from cut-price failures to true connoisseur choices.

WHO LOVED IT?

The TL1000, initially at least, was an unmitigated disaster, prompting its deletion after only four years. Today, however, particularly for its lusty engine, it's regarded as an appreciating, misunderstood modern classic.

YAMAHA YZF-R1, 1998

Yamaha's R1 was the last great superbike revolution of the 1990s thanks to its ultra-compact size, light weight and class-leading power. The FireBlade had finally been dethroned. (Yamaha)

If Honda's 1992 CBR900RR FireBlade rewrote the superbike rule book, emphasising light weight and compactness over raw power, then the 1998 Yamaha R1 proved lightning can strike twice by establishing a new benchmark for power, light weight and control and, in so doing, set the template for all superbikes that followed. Even today, an original R1 is a competitive, credible and impressive superbike.

Although unveiled with a glittering fanfare at the 1997 Milan Show, when factory rider Scott Russell rode the bike on stage wearing a silver suit with a backdrop illuminated only with the then revolutionary figures of 150bhp and 177kg, the R1's story had begun a full eighteen months earlier, at the launch of its predecessor, the YZF1000R Thunderace in South Africa.

The R1 was publicly unveiled at the Milan Show the previous November, where it was ridden on stage by a silver-suited Scott Russell with the backdrop simply proclaiming 150bhp and 177kg. (Yamaha)

There, Project Leader Kunihiko Miwa, already aware that the 'Ace was too heavy and cumbersome to be a true superbike contender (it was actually pitched as a 'supersport tourer'), began sketching out his ideas for a revolutionary new machine.

One key element, derived from his experiences in 500 GPs, was for a 'stacked' gearbox that allowed the engine to be unusually short. This in turn allowed a short wheelbase for nimble handling but also a long swingarm to help stability and prevent wheelies.

WHAT THEY SAID

'The Yamaha has two invaluable but less definable qualities that are almost impossible to consciously build into – it has character and it is fun to ride and that combined with its stunning performance make it unquestionably the best production road sports bike ever built.'

Superbike magazine, March 1998, on the £9,459 Yamaha YZF-R1

The resulting short engine in turn enabled a short wheelbase for nimble handling yet, crucially, allowed retention of the long swingarm necessary for suspension control and to counteract wheelies. (Yamaha)

The R1's radical engine design was key: although a familiar five-valve transverse four, it was ultra-compact thanks to a novel 'stacked gearbox' design developed from grand prix practice. (Yamaha)

Even the R1's instrument display was revolutionary. Although the analogue revcounter was conventional, Yamaha's new superbike was the first to feature a digital LCD speedometer. (Yamaha)

The overall result, as revealed at its world press launch in the US, raised the bar for both ultra-nimble yet secure superbike handling and high-power explosive performance. (Yamaha)

WHO LOVED IT?

The R1 was one of the most successful bikes of the late 1990s. It was thereafter successively updated and became established as Yamaha's flagship sports bike. Original 1998 machines are now sought-after modern classics.

This, combined with a series of weight-reduction measures, added up to a bike that was more powerful than the FireBlade, 5kg lighter and 10mm shorter, and resulted in a bike that, on track, simply blew all comers away and ruled the roost for the rest of the decade, so claiming the crown as the ultimate sports bike of the 1990s. It wasn't finally usurped until the first GSX-R1000 arrived in 2001.

Even then that wasn't the end of the R1 story. Miwa followed it up in 1999 with an equally radical little brother, the 600cc R6, which proved just as revolutionary in supersports, and the R1 was successively updated, comprehensively establishing itself as Yamaha's new superbike king. Its most recent WSB crown came in 2021.

Today, original 1998 R1s are considered collectable modern classics, while R1 creator Miwa is as revered as the FireBlade's creator Tadao Baba.

The first year 1998 YZF-R1 was available in solid Yamaha blue or the Japanese firm's traditional white and red racing colours. The latter was the most popular but, either way, a new king was born. (Yamaha)

SUZUKI GSX-1300R HAYABUSA, 1999

Suzuki's 'final hurrah' of the 1990s was its attempt to wrest the 'world's fastest production bike' crown away from Honda's CBR1100XX Super Blackbird. The astonishing GSX-1300R Hayabusa was the result. (Suzuki)

If the 1990s began with a new breed of hyperbike, Kawasaki's ZZ-R1100, which set a new standard for speed, the decade ended, appropriately enough, with the last word on the subject – Suzuki's GSX-1300R Hayabusa.

Just as Honda's 1996 CBR1100XX Super Blackbird had set out to wrest the 'king of speed' crown from the ZZ-R, the Hayabusa was created to do the same to the CBR. Even its name, Hayabusa, was that of a Japanese falcon that preyed on blackbirds …

Suzuki took no half measures in its creation, either. Its all-new four-cylinder engine was a huge 1298cc that, with ram air, produced a massive 175bhp. Its long, low-slung, aluminium, twin-spar chassis was massive, too, chiefly for stability in a straight line. But most radical of all was the 'Busa's ultra-aerodynamic, wind tunnel-developed bodywork. No 1990s bike looked so distinctive or went so fast – and that proved its ending, too.

An all-new design based around a massive, 1,298cc four-cylinder engine, the GSX-1300R also had an immensely sturdy and stable all-new twin-beam frame. (Suzuki)

WHAT THEY SAID

'It's quite, quite mad but a real pussycat to ride. It'll only try to kill you or rearrange your concept of what is fast if you ask it to.'

Superbike magazine, April 1999, on the £7,999 GSX-1300R Hayabusa

And, with 175bhp and striking, ultra-aerodynamic, wind tunnel-developed bodywork, the Hayabusa was instantly proven to be the fastest bike available. (Suzuki)

WHO LOVED IT?

The 'first-gen' Hayabusa quickly became known as the world's fastest production motorcycle, sold well and developed a devoted following. Some 60,760 examples of the first iteration were made up to 2004.

Early versions were routinely tested at over 190mph, some nudging 200. Scare stories started appearing and, before the decade was out, the Japanese 'Big Four' manufacturers reportedly made a 'gentleman's agreement' to curtail the sensationalist speed race by enacting a voluntary 300kph (187mph) limit. The Hayabusa wasn't only the fastest bike of the 1990s. It was the fastest bike for all time. Maybe.

Of course, there was more to the Hayabusa than that. It was a capable hyper-tourer, it was classy and popular, and it generated a devoted following that would last through three incarnations up to this day. But 'fastest' remains a massive part of its appeal – and probably always will.

YAMAHA YZF-R6, 1999

If the R1 was Yamaha's first new 'R' machine, it was soon obvious that it wasn't to be the last. The year 1999 saw the arrival of its equally radical 600cc little brother, the YZF-R6. (Yamaha)

Just as Yamaha's R1 revolutionised superbike with its compactness and sheer speed, its little brother, the 600cc R6, did exactly the same in supersports a year later.

But where the R1 used radical technology, the R6 instead brought a focus and top-quality components 600cc bikes hadn't seen before. Until the R6, supersports machines were slightly compromised all-rounders with one eye on value. Afterwards, they were hardcore sports weapons that could give 750s a run for their money and gave a whole new generation access to 160mph speed.

To achieve that, the R6 used exactly the same concepts as the R1, with an aluminium Deltabox frame, high-revving, four-cylinder engine producing 118bhp at 13,000rpm, compact, lightweight dimensions that gave ultra-nimble handling plus quality brakes and suspension. The result looked like a racer, went like a racer and got the results of a racer, winning countless supersport titles around the globe. The R6 also forced all rivals to follow suit with the raciest yet, Kawasaki ZX-6R and all-new Honda CBR600RR, not long in its wake.

This time available in red, white, black or blue, the R6, like its bigger sibling, was a no-compromise, ultra-compact, high-power sportster that brought new levels of performance to the supersports class. (Yamaha)

WHAT THEY SAID

'If you're looking for a bike that rewards aggressive riding and sick of paying for 1000cc insurance the R6 might just be the ticket.'

Superbike magazine, March 1999, on the £6,599 Yamaha YZF-R6

Capable of 160mph and with nimble racetrack handling, the R6 brought superbike-style performance within the budget and reach of a generation of supersport buyers. (Yamaha)

The 1999 Yamaha R6 may not have been the most popular, versatile or affordable supersports 600 of the 1990s, but it was the fastest and the one that changed the direction of the whole class.

After the arrival of the R6, never again would supersports bikes be compromised all-rounders, as proven by the arrival in the early 2000s of Honda's MotoGP-style CBR600RR and others. (Yamaha)

WHO LOVED IT?

Launched on the coat-tails of the even more revolutionary R1, the R6 was the most extreme supersports 600 of the 1990s, loved for its raw, peaky purity and with handling and performance that raised the class bar.

MV AGUSTA F4 750, 1999

If there was a prize for the most exotic, beautiful, exclusive and desirable superbike of the 1990s, the MV Agusta F4 750 would surely be it.

The dream project of the family business that earlier rescued Ducati, designed by the genius who came up with the Ducati 916 and bearing the most revered name in Italian motorcycling history, the first bike of the revived MV concern had it all – or rather, it nearly did.

In 1996 Cagiva shocked the world by selling Ducati. A few years later it became clear why. Having bought the defunct but historic MV Agusta brand in 1992, it launched its first new MV in 1999, the F4 750. (MV Agusta)

After buying and reviving Ducati in the late 1980s and early '90s with bikes like the Monster and 916, Claudio Castiglioni's Cagiva surprisingly sold the Bologna marque in 1996. But what many didn't know then was that he had bought up the rights to the historic, defunct MV Agusta brand in 1991 and had even bigger ambitions.

WHAT THEY SAID

'Try as you might, you can't rule out a bike like the MV, no matter how exclusive and expensive it becomes. People always want special but the simple lack of production and spares availability is a major drawback.'

Bike magazine, December 2002, on the £12,300 MV Agusta F4 S

The first bike was the F4 750, an all-new, three-quarter-litre superbike following MV's four-cylinder heritage but one fit for the twenty-first century. On paper it had everything going for it: an engine co-developed with Ferrari; the very best cycle parts money could buy; and, most glorious of all, styling by Massimo Tamburini that seemed a step up even from his 916 and including another single-sided swingarm and no fewer than *four* under-seat exhausts.

The brainchild of Cagiva boss Claudio Castiglioni, the new MV F4 was designed and styled by Massimo Tamburini, who'd previously designed the Ducati 916. It was a more than worthy successor. (MV Agusta)

In many ways the F4 was an evolution of the 916: a transverse four instead of a V-twin; a composite tubular steel frame with cast-alloy sections, the same single-sided swingarm and four under-seat exhausts. It had it all. (MV Agusta)

The F4 was unveiled in limited edition 'Serio Oro' form at Monza's historic banked circuit. But although beautiful, innovative, fast and fine handling, it was also expensive and plagued by problems. (MV Agusta)

It went as well as it looked – ultra-focused and extreme with a screaming 126bhp. Unfortunately, production difficulties and delays meant that, by the time the F4 came to market, the arrival of Suzuki's 128bhp GSX-R750 SRAD and Yamaha's more powerful (and lighter) R1 meant the new MV was out-performed before it had even been launched. Worse, it was prohibitively expensive, dealers were scarce and production faced countless problems, all of which devastated Castiglioni's MV dream.

As a 'motorcycle made art' and an ultra-desirable class, however, nothing then – or still – comes close.

WHO LOVED IT?

Beautiful, fast and bearing one of the most historic names in biking, everyone loved the F4 750 even if few could justify buying it. Immediately outpaced by Suzuki's GSX-R750, just a few thousand F4 750s were built (including 300 first-edition 'Serie Oro' models) before evolving into the F4 1000.

YAMAHA YZF-R7, 1999

Another stupendous 750cc superbike of the late 1990s also 'had it all'. The homologation special YZF-R7 (or OW-02) was Yamaha's successor to the Japanese firm's OW-01. (Yamaha)

Yamaha's 1999 R7 homologation special racer built to compete in the World Superbike Championship has another, more internal designation that tells you all you need to know about the last and arguably greatest 750cc superbike of the 1990s: OW-02.

As such it combined everything Yamaha had learned about four-cylinder performance, blended it with the very best components available and wrapped it in arguably the most beautiful Japanese sports-bike bodywork ever.

The result had a five-valve, 749cc four capable of 160bhp (but we'll get back to that); bespoke aluminium Deltabox twin-beam frame with adjustable everything; top-spec, multi-adjustable Ohlins forks and rear shock; while lightweight wheels, tank and more added up to a dry weight of just 176kg. To you: £22,000.

As a road bike, of course, although exquisite, it wasn't quite that good. In road trim it produced just 106bhp, with the 55 extra horses only available via a £10,000 race kit, while on track, although the best of the Japanese fours, it never delivered the World Superbike crown hoped for it.

Like its predecessor, the R7 was designed purely for racetrack glory, featured everything Yamaha then knew about five-valve, four-cylinder performance and was produced in very limited quantities. (Yamaha)

Unfortunately, although exquisite and more than capable, the R7, too, never overcame the capacity advantage of Ducati's all-dominant 1000cc V-twin in WSB and elsewhere. (Yamaha)

WHAT THEY SAID

'Have Yamaha produced the bike of the Millennium? Well, yes and no. No because, as standard, it's restricted to 106bhp and because there are going to be just 500 of the buggers built. And, yes, because it is without question the most advanced production bike ever built.'

Superbike magazine, May 1999, on the £22,000 Yamaha YZF-R7

To a large degree, though, that doesn't matter. The R7 remains, still, the ultimate incarnation of the Japanese 750cc four-cylinder sportster and one of the rarest and most desirable bikes of the 1990s, if not of all time. No bike was better suited to round off the decade.

But as a glorious 'ultimate' of the late 1990s, the Yamaha R7 still provided a fitting epitaph to the decade and remains one of the most desirable and exclusive Japanese superbikes to this day. (Yamaha)

WHO LOVED IT?

Only ever intended as a limited production homologation special, just the required 500 examples of the YZF-R7 were built, with only forty of those being brought to the UK.